The College Football Book

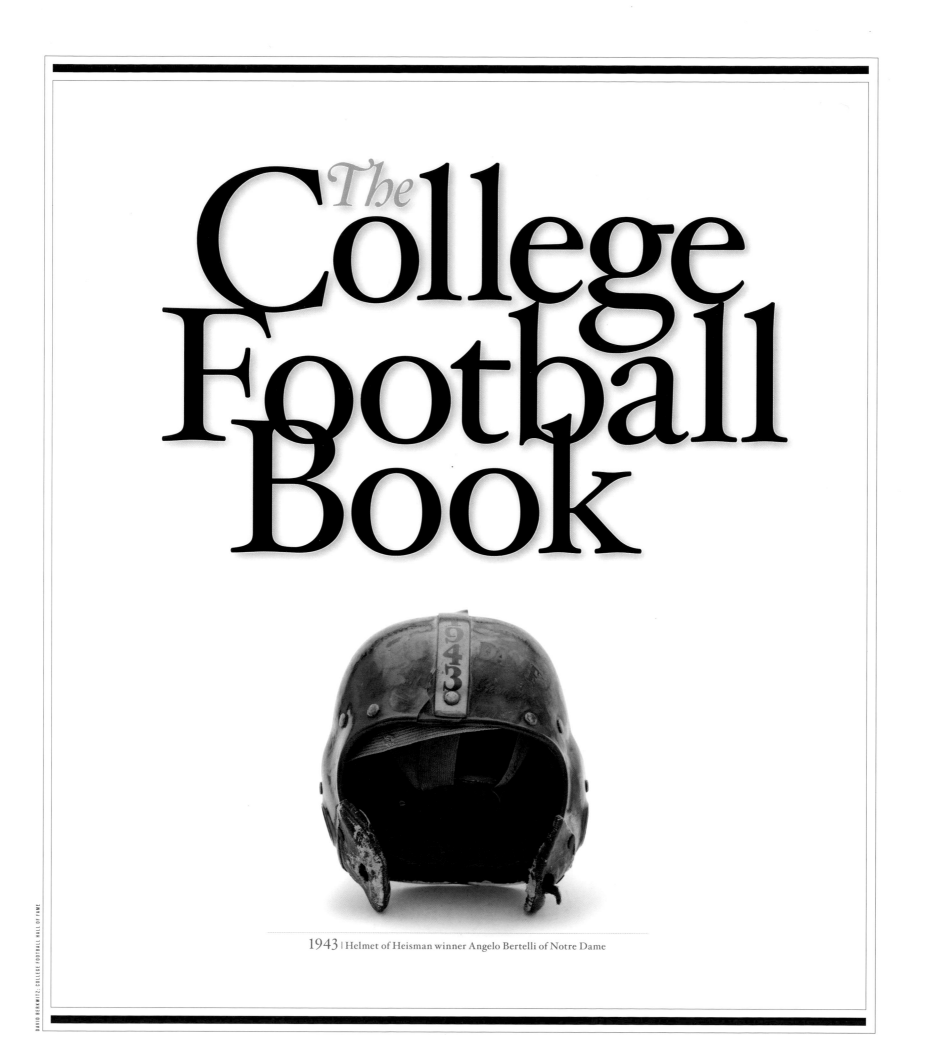

1943 | Helmet of Heisman winner Angelo Bertelli of Notre Dame

TIME TO PLAY

MIN. SEC.

SYRACUSE 0:00 T.C.U.

DOWN YDS. TO GO QUARTER

FIRST NATIONAL BANK IN DALLAS

WELCOME COTTON BOWL DALLAS WELCOME COTTON BOWL DALLAS WELCOME COTTON BOWL DALLAS

1957 | MODERN GLADIATORS, the Syracuse Orangemen, including star halfbacks Jim Ridlon (16) and Jim Brown (not visible here), entered the arena for their Cotton Bowl game against TCU. | *Photograph by* MARVIN E. NEWMAN

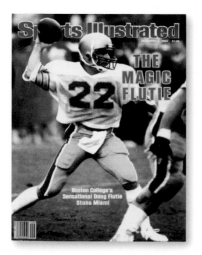

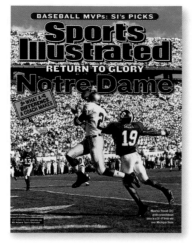

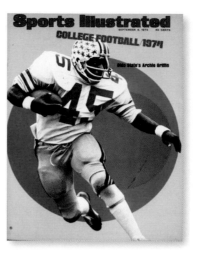

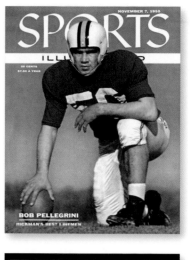

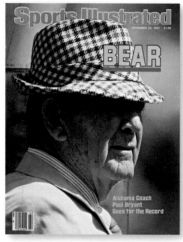

The College Football Book

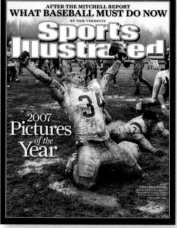

ROB FLEDER
Editor

STEVEN HOFFMAN
Designer

DICK FRIEDMAN *Senior Editor*   DAVID SABINO *Associate Editor*

CRISTINA SCALET *Photo Editor*   JENNIFER GRAD *Assistant Photo Editor*

KEVIN KERR *Copy Editor*   JOSH DENKIN *Associate Designer*

ADAM DUERSON *Reporter*

THE COLLEGE FOOTBALL HALL OF FAME
Archives and Historical Reference

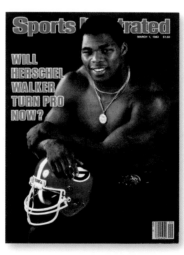

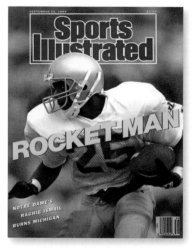

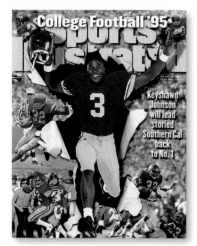

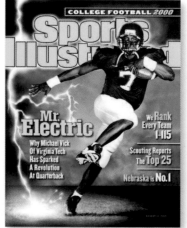

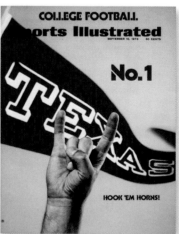

![Sports Illustrated]

Contents

1881 | WALTER CAMP (seated, front left) got a foothold as football's father when he was captain of an unbeaten Yale team. | *Photograph by* BROWN BROTHERS

1883 | WITH A 6–0 win over Princeton at the
Polo Grounds, Yale was on the road to the national
championship. | *Photograph by* DAVID BERKWITZ

1981 | A TRIUMPH over archrival Auburn put
Alabama's Bear Bryant alone at the top of the alltime list
of career coaching wins. | *Photograph by* DAVID BERKWITZ

9

2005 | HURDLING TOWARD the end zone and a Heisman, Southern Cal's Reggie Bush went airborne to evade UCLA's Marcus Cassel. | *Photograph by* PETER READ MILLER

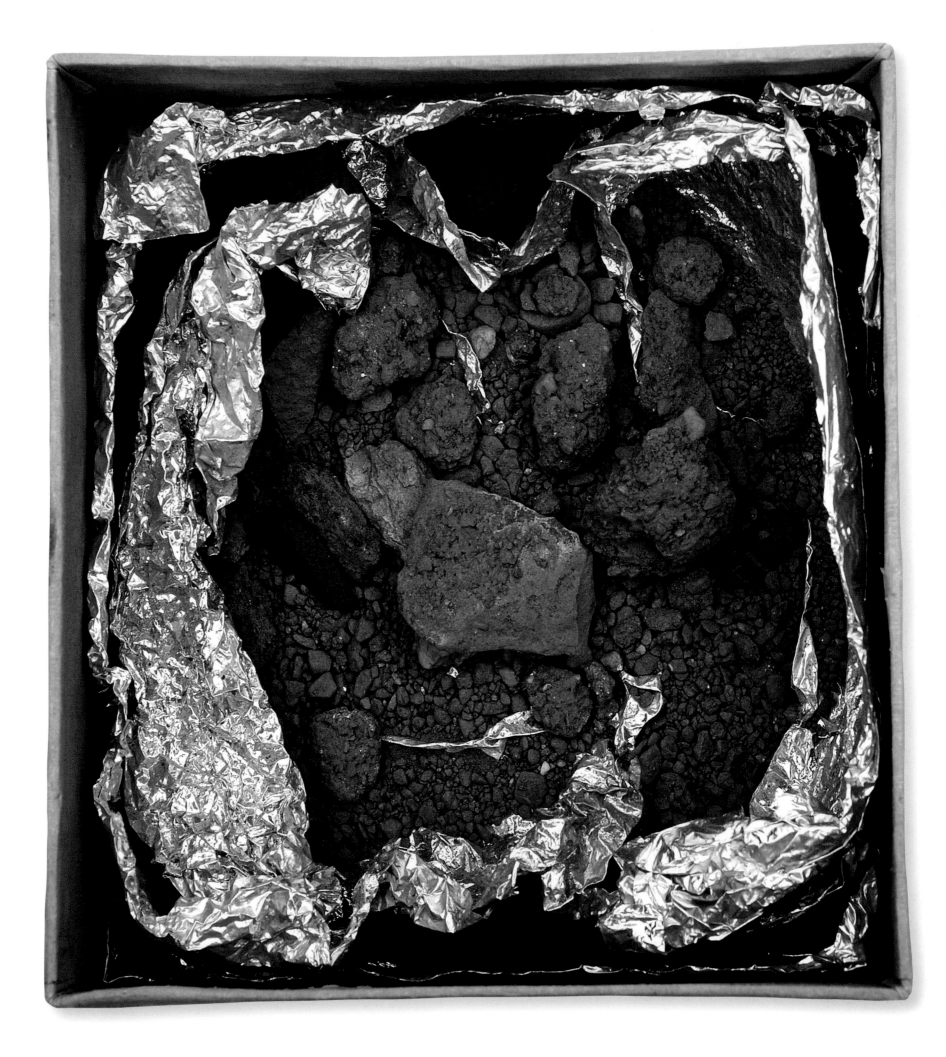

INTRODUCTION
BY RICK TELANDER

IF YOU PLAYED COLLEGE FOOTBALL

YOU LIKELY HAVE SOME SCARS TO SHOW FOR IT. I'VE GOT A BENT LEFT RING FINGER. I DESERVED IT FOR GRABBING A RUNNING BACK'S JERSEY RATHER THAN FOLLOWING THE DEFENSIVE COACH'S ORDERS, THE TACKLING INSTRUCTIONS HOLLERED IN PRACTICE SO OFTEN THAT THE WORDS FLOATED PAST LIKE POLLEN IN THE BREEZE:

"PUT YOUR HAT ON HIM!"

HALLOWED GROUND from the field on which Rutgers beat Princeton in 1869 now resides in the Hall of Fame, an elemental link to the modern game.

My buddy, the middle linebacker, did put his hat on a fullback from Indiana one time, rolling blindly off a block into the runner's churning thigh. When my pal came to, not long after the collision, he spent some time on hands and knees looking for his mouthpiece in the blades of turf at Bloomington's Memorial Stadium. Problem was, he hadn't been wearing a mouthpiece. And, as I suggested to him later, had he been wearing one, it would have to have been the size of a dental filling to disappear in that plastic carpet.

The point is that college football is just the wildest, noisiest, most concussive thing going on when you're in it, and when you come out of it what you've got are some old wounds and a bunch of memories. Even now, nearly four decades after my last game, my memories are as vivid as sparklers: the pregame motel steak that I was too nervous to eat; Joe Zigulich's long snaps coming at me like spinning missiles when I was Northwestern's punter my junior year; the mortar between the bricks in the tunnel at Notre Dame Stadium; the Southern Cal receiver's shoulder pads flapping as he ran up the left sideline—my sideline—at the Los Angeles Coliseum; the sportswriters with their notepads coming sheeplike into our locker room after losses; the piles of dirty tape on the floor resembling the shed skins of molting reptiles. It may be one of the mysteries of the great American game that the memories of playing college football actually seem to get more vivid as time goes on.

And yet, what a player sees out there on the field is wildly different from what everyone else sees. Witnesses are important, but when there are more than about 30,000 of them, the crowd disappears. It becomes a quivering backdrop of dull color and muffled sound. Cheerleaders, mascots, police, dancing girls—all gone. A facade. The game is so powerful and so riveting that you are blinded to all but your assignments, your keys, your coach, your man. You see as if through the wrong end of a telescope. The chaos and compartmentalization is such that you really do need to watch the film to know what happened.

Which brings up the beauty of this book. So *that's* what Jim Plunkett's *(page 42)* drop-back looks like! *That's* what Barry Sanders *(page 144)* looks like frozen in mid-air! *That's* how a blocked man *(page 82)* looks at impact!

When you're playing the game, there's no time to savor anything. But these photos and interspersed stories are here for our endless savoring.

So much has changed in the 139 years since the first game was played by students from Princeton and Rutgers, turbans on their heads, minds charged by manly and nostalgic tales of the recently ended Civil War, that it's a wonder there's a common thread at all. But a simple box of dirt from the field where that first contest was held—25 men to a side, round ball, no passing, little strategy, lots of kicking and violence—has the power to link anyone who has ever felt the essential (yes, primitive) lure of the sport. I mean: dirt. Even at Ohio State, even at Nebraska, even with Dick Butkus comin' at you, with Earl Campbell lowering his big helmet at the goal line, dirt is as pure as it gets.

So much was already there in that first game that can't be accounted for simply by developments in rules or equipment or strategy. For instance, the Rutgers and Princeton lads genuinely seemed to dislike one another and wanted to use the game not just to prove their athletic dominance but also to pummel the other side. According to a newspaper interview many years later with William Preston Lane, one of the Princeton players, the victorious Rutgers team "ran us Princeton men out of town." Lane meant that literally: "When we saw them coming after us, we ran to the outskirts of New Brunswick and got into our carriages and wagons and went away as fast as we could."

This may be hyperbole. But it is a fact that after the two teams played for a second time that year, administrators from both institutions prevented a third game from taking place because this sudden "over-emphasis" on football was interfering with the educational mission of the universities. Wow,

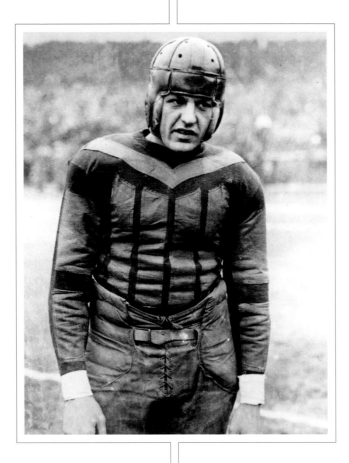

A LEGEND in his own time, Illinois's Red Grange embodied college football's galloping popularity in the 1920s and paved the way for the icons who followed.

where'd they think that one up? But you know and I know that college football was off and rolling, and the beast would never again be put back in its cage.

Indeed, I thought college football was huge when I was playing it in the late 1960s and early '70s. That was the era of Woody and Bo and Bear, after all, and a place like the entire state of Alabama pretty much came to a stop every Saturday when the Crimson Tide was rolling over some hapless foe. But those days, like everything else in America, were nothing compared to what was coming. Thirty million people attended college football games in 1971; by 2006 almost 48 million did. And that doesn't count the increase in TV watchers, a figure that has gone plain nutty. Stats are boring, but consider this: 129 million households watched bowl games in '07-08. I'm no math wizard, but if there were two or three people in each of those households, that's pretty much the population of the United States right there. Oh, we do love college football! We love the colors and the tailgating and the marching bands and the alma maters and the rivalries and the autumn ritual of throwing minifootballs in parking lots and thinking we're all happy campus kids once again.

But the "amateur" game has grown so much that its quasi-professionalism is hardly distinguishable from the NFL's full-blown capitalistic onslaught. I look at my old Northwestern media guide and see that the Wildcats played more than nine games in a regular season only once from 1908 to '64. When I arrived in Evanston in '67 we, like most of the teams in the Big Ten, played 10 regular-season games, and only one conference team each year went to a bowl game, the Rose Bowl. (In 2007–08, eight of the 11 Big Ten teams went to a bowl game.) College football has blown past the 10-game season so that now every team plays at least a dozen games, with some playing as many as 14. But you know America—if a little is good, a lot is better. And it's hard to imagine how much college football would be too much for us.

The heroes of the past—Grange, Brown, Namath,

Dorsett, Walker—have dissolved easily into the heroes of recent memory: Moss, Faulk, Young, Bush, Russell. A lot of the early pedestal-building was done by sportswriters who saw in the tumult of the game the raw materials of mythology. Take a gander at Grantland Rice's Underwood typewriter (*page 17*), a dark, dense cube of metal and ink so ponderous and inert it could be melted down into pig iron. And yet he used it as a poet's quill on parchment. With that monster, newspaperman Rice clacked out columns that took the Four Horsemen of the Apocalypse and turned them into . . . trumpets, please . . . the offensive backfield quartet from Notre Dame! Famine, Pestilence, Destruction, Death? Who they? We're talking Harry Stuhldreher and his posse! Why, the Book of Revelation was no doubt written just so sportswriters could compare Barry Switzer's option offense to a plague of locusts.

Here's where I guess I have to plead guilty myself, because once I left the college playing fields and put away childish things—such as living in a massive, debauched, off-campus house with a half-dozen depraved former NU football jocks like myself—I became a sports scribe and continued the mythologizing. At first I wrote freelance pieces for various publications, then I wrote for SPORTS ILLUSTRATED itself, covering the very sport I once had played. It was weird at times. The smells, the passions, the tingles—I experienced them all as I returned to campuses and covered young men who reminded me of so many things I'd been a part of. One day I went with just-hired Ohio State coach John Cooper to inspect the piece of wooded property in Columbus, where he planned to build his coach's mansion. A woodchuck, or maybe a big squirrel, darted near an oak tree, and I told Cooper it was a wolverine. The man looked so horrified, I felt bad for even leading him on for a moment. Oh, the passions of the Woody-Bo conflict! They have led, even without us writers turning up the voltage, to glorious electrical storms that pit not only one school against another, but one state against another,

THE AUTHOR still carries vivid memories—and a variety of scars—from his glory days as a defensive back at Northwestern four decades ago.

one way of life against another. When I see a photo of the Georgia bulldog, Uga IV, lying, panting, on a bag of ice on page 76 of this book, I know it is because it does get muggy down there in Athens. But the heat of the biggest rivalries—Ohio State–Michigan, Texas-Oklahoma, Florida–Florida State, UCLA-USC, even Harvard-Yale—makes that pooch a symbol of all the revved-up college players and coaches and fans everywhere.

Things change in college football—face masks, muscles, area codes on eye-black patches—but the essence never does. Football is a game boys invented because boys like to kick the crud out of each other, and when you throw organization and TV and money and cheering and the American educational system into the mix, well, you've got a guaranteed, growth-oriented whoop-de-do on your hands.

Some of the changes in the game, of course, reflect social developments that reach far beyond the field. I look back at my freshman team at Northwestern (freshmen weren't allowed on the varsity, remember): 32 players, two managers, three graduate assistants, one head coach—and not one black face. This was 1967, not 1907. I find it amazing. In fact I found it amazing even as I was playing with that pale squad. In '69 Texas would win the national championship with an all-white team, and that would seem bizarre too. Where, for God's sake, were the black guys? When integration finally arrived everywhere on the football field, a lot of things changed. Mentor-teachers like Eddie Robinson at Grambling (*page 134*) would no longer have to be the saviors for great talent denied opportunity. And its arrival would help fuel the game's rocketing growth. Up, up, up. How about that—black fellows can even play quarterback! Who would have thunk it?

I wonder more these days about smaller issues in college football, things that are not quite so sweeping in their significance. Will the constant pressure of money-making and championship-seeking ruin the kids? Will millionaire coaches sully the legacy of the middle-class coaches of olden times? Will the grass stain finally be eliminated forever by the artificial turf burn and the ground-up-tire pellets clinging to

socks? Will players stay on campus, lifting and running and film-studying, and never leave the athletic fortress, ever? I wonder, as old-timers are wont to do, about the "innocence" of the game being lost to ceaseless pressure to entertain. But I've read my football history. Teddy Roosevelt worried about all that too, a century ago.

I'm sure there won't be many more write-ups like mine from the 1968 Northwestern media guide, a pamphlet as small and colorless as a motel notepad: "Rick's performance during the spring established him as the top receiving prospect among the sophomores-to-be. He has excellent moves for working his way into the open, and his better than average speed makes him an open-field threat. He's conversant with the throwing end of a pass, too, having played quarterback and end in high school. . . ."

Seeing *conversant* used in something other than a discussion of languages is worth a chuckle. And this "open-field threat" was quickly turned into a defensive back, where I would remain for the rest of my collegiate days. The highlight of my career came against Ohio State when, as a senior cornerback, I intercepted two Rex Kern passes in the first half at Ohio Stadium. But we lost that game, and thus, the Big Ten championship, and the No.2–ranked Buckeyes would be the one and only bowl participant from our conference. And so it would pretty much end for me.

That's why seeing the photograph of Stanford's Plunkett dropping back to throw against Ohio State in that 1971 Rose Bowl is painful. The Buckeyes had such a primitive passing attack themselves that they weren't very good defending against Stanford's air offense, and they were upset 27–17. I have always felt that if Northwestern had gone to that Rose Bowl, we would have done a better job than Ohio State. Aw, who knows. Probably not. Just an old grump talking about what might have been. But as I said at the start, you've got your scars and you need to see the film to figure it all out.

I can study this book for a long time and learn things I thought I knew or had never quite learned at all. Yes, sometimes the sky really was that blue. Sometimes the light was that pure, that warm, that full of life. ꙮ

AN EPIC poet of the press box, Rice banged out mass-market mythology on his Underwood, none more deathless than his Four Horsemen column in 1924.

The College

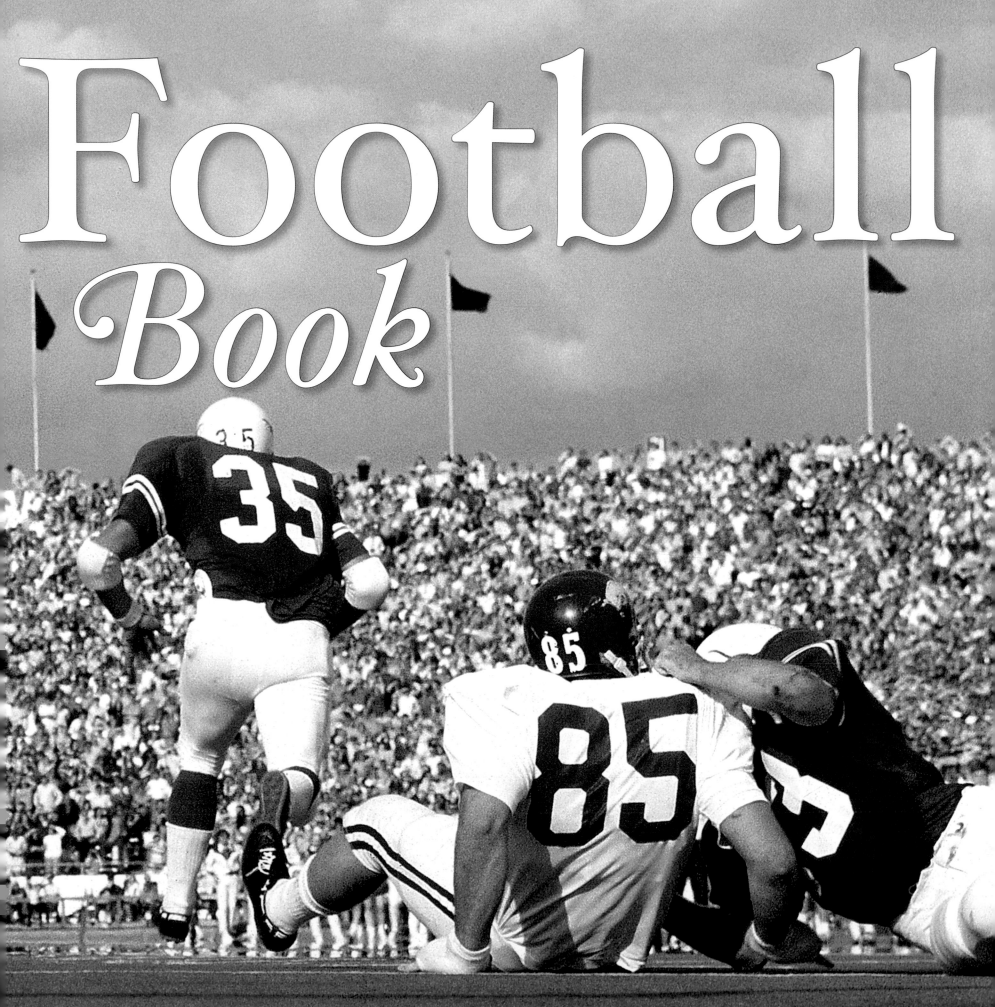

Football *Book*

1970 | JIM BERTELSEN of top-ranked Texas had nothing but blue skies ahead as he steamed upfield in the Longhorns' 42–7 rout of Arkansas. | *Photograph by* WALTER IOOSS JR.

1937 | THE NEARLY angelic countenance of rugged Mississippi All-America tackle Frank Kinard gave no hint of his nickname: Bruiser. | *Photograph by* PICTORIAL PARADE

1980 | BAR NONE, Pittsburgh's end Hugh Green had the highest finish (second) for a purely defensive player in Heisman voting. | *Photograph by* GEORGE GOJKOVICH

2003 | NOTRE DAME'S Rhema McKnight somehow snagged this throw, but staying in bounds was too much of a stretch during a 29–26 overtime win by the Fighting Irish over Washington State. | *Photograph by* JOE ROBBINS

'I DO LOVE THE FOOTBALL'

BY FRANK DEFORD

After 43 years of coaching and 314 wins, Bear Bryant's passion for the game was undiminished. —*from* SI, NOVEMBER 23, 1981

THE PIGSKIN HISTORIAN begins to sort through the mounds of evidence that are supposed to add up to the man who is identified as coach Paul (Bear) Bryant. It is all there, in layers, by now a folk chronicle, each tale told and retold in nearly the same language every time, and all irrespective of relative importance, time or place: The Bear and his humble origins in Moro Bottom, near Fordyce, Ark.; The Bear at Alabama as "the other end" opposite the immortal Don Hutson; the tales of how The Bear got his name (accounts provided by every possible eyewitness, save perhaps the noble ursine itself); The Bear and the bowls; The Bear and the record—Amos Alonzo Stagg's 314 victories as a coach, which Bryant tied last Saturday with a 31–16 defeat of Penn State and could surpass next week against Auburn; The Bear that first hellish summer in Aggieland; The Bear returns to his Alabama; The Bear and his hat; The Bear and The Baron; The Bear walks on water (and other fables); the ages of The Bear.

By now, it is all so blurred yet all so neat. The more one reads—the more one suffers through the same stuff from The Bear and his hagiographers—the more one understands a friend of The Bear's, a Tuscaloosa physician, who says, "That he mumbles really doesn't matter to me anymore, because by now, I always know what he is going to say, anyway."

But, what have we here? Tucked deep into the recesses of another bio folder, there is one other obscure clipping, from a time long ago. It seems, studying this scrap of parchment, that as yet another Honor America Day approached, a certain U.S. politician named Nixon was beleaguered, beset on all sides by his bloodthirsty foes. But, after months of holing up, he decided that Honor America Day would be an appropriate occasion on which to launch a counterattack, to venture out again and reach for the souls of decent citizens. And so, he would go forth and deliver a speech.

And here, from *The New York Times*, is the last paragraph of that story: "Invitations to attend the celebration were also sent to John Wayne, the actor; Paul Harvey, the news broadcaster; Billy Graham, the evangelist; and Paul (Bear) Bryant, the University of Alabama football coach."

At that time The Bear had 231 wins and was counting.

THE FIRST of the two-a-days in the 24th year of coach Paul (Bear) Bryant's tenure at Alabama takes place just after dawn on a steamy summer's day, Monday, Aug. 17. It will be winter, four and a half months later, before the Crimson Tide is finished playing; the team has gone to a bowl for 22 straight years and, by now, as The Bear says, "We win two games, some bowl will invite us."

Where The Bear now has his football offices, in Memorial Coliseum, adjoining the practice complex, was all cotton fields when he first arrived in Tuscaloosa, coming over from the bottom country of Arkansas. It was the fall of '31, the Depression, and the segregated South was like a different nation then—one party, one crop, one sport and one dollar if you were lucky. "There wasn't but about three cars on campus then," The Bear recalls, exaggerating only a little bit. Now, as dawn breaks, his players drive up in all manner of vehicles; hardly a one walks the half mile from the dormitory.

The Bear meets briefly with his team—alone. "You wouldn't want someone else to sit in when you talked private with your wife, would you?" he says. Occasionally, he drives home this point in somewhat earthier terms. He's still very close to his boys. He doesn't sleep over at the dormitory anymore, the way Joe Namath remembers, but there is still a tight bond. "I get so tired of it at times," The Bear admits. "But I do love the football, the contact with my players. I still get a thrill outta jes' goin' to practice. Jes' steppin' out there. I do. That's my hobby." Another thing he says regularly when strangers ask even innocuous questions about his players, is this. "I wouldn't know, and I wouldn't tell you if I did."

The Bear puts on his baseball cap now, for practice. He is about the last man who has his hair and still wears a hat

TWO BEAR trademarks, the houndstooth hat and the unyielding visage, were prominent in '66, when 'Bama was the nation's only undefeated, untied team.

all the time. Outside of coach Paul (Bear) Bryant down in Alabama, you can tell bald men this way: They are the ones wearing hats. But if The Bear still has hair, it isn't so curly and bright as it used to be, so his jug ears stand out more. In fact he can look very old sometimes, away from the sideline stripes. He is wrinkled and gray and his coat rides up high on his neck and his pants droop off his seat, and he just shuffles along. He looks, for example, a lot older than President Reagan, who is, at 70, two and a half years his senior. "Yeah, but the President ain't run around and drank anywhere near so much whiskey as The Bear," a friend says. That's probably true, although not necessarily to the benefit of the ship of state.

The moon is gone now and the sun is up for the first of the two-a-days, and The Bear strides through the guarded tunnel that goes from the coliseum to the practice fields, under a fence topped with barbed wire and masked with high shrubs. And now The Bear is different. He is some kind of different. He is coach Paul (Bear) Bryant, and he seems an altogether new man, a whole lot younger.

Now he begins to trudge up the 33 steps to the top of the tower, where a chair, a bullhorn and a can of bug spray await him. The latter is for some hornets up there who don't appreciate what place the man in the tower holds in the human kingdom. He peers down on all his players. There are almost 130, counting the walk-ons, all in color-coded shirts—red for the first offense, white for first defense, blue, green, yellow and orange—looking like game pieces on some great, green, white-striped board. The Gridiron King will zero in on this one or that one for two or three plays, but, of course, nobody down there knows whom he might be watching at any given moment. He'll just all of a sudden yell out, "Nice catch," or "Straight up, straight up," or "You can't run any faster than that, get your ass outta here," or "Come on, come on, start showin' some class. Fourth quarter now, fourth quarter." But everybody feels The Bear is coming right down on him, which is the way he wants it.

The Bear says, "When I first came here I was fightin' for my life out there on the field. Well, I'm still fightin' for my life. It's just that I don't have near as many years left."

By the time coach Paul (Bear) Bryant got back to Alabama, age 44, in 1958, he had already accumulated 91 coaching victories at Maryland, Kentucky and Texas A&M, places on the fringes of Dixie. Now he was returning to his alma mater, to home, and in the very year that C. Vann Woodward, the distinguished Southern historian, was making this observation. "The time is coming, if indeed it as not already arrived, when the Southerner will begin to ask himself whether there is really any longer very much point in calling himself a Southerner." How could C. Vann Woodward know that, 23 years later, The Bear would be going for 315?

The Bear is meaningful. That is his legacy—not just so many more victories. History has always been important to the South, and The Bear is a historical figure. It was right after another victory last month, number 310, and Billy Varner, his driver, had just spirited him away in the Buick LeSabre, two motorcycle cops running ahead through the traffic, their blue lights flashing, when someone was moved to say, "They'll sure never be another Bear." And the writer from the campus newspaper, an Alabama boy, said, "Well, not unless there's another Civil War." And that is pretty much it. For Alabama, anyway, The Bear is triumph, at last; even more than that, he is justification.

> FOR ALABAMA, ANYWAY, THE BEAR IS TRIUMPH. HE IS JUSTIFICATION. HE IS ONE OF THEIR VERY OWN GOOD OLD BOYS WHO TOOK ON THE REST OF THE NATION AND WHIPPED IT.

The Bear hates all that joking about him being some sort of Dixie Christ (his card-playing friends at Indian Hills Country Club refer to him as "Old Water-Walker"—behind his back), and he's right to, for whether or not it's sacrilege, it's bad theology. The Bear is very human. That is the point. He is one of their own good old boys who took on the rest of the nation and whipped it. The wisest thing that The Bear never did was to run against George Wallace for governor, not so much because he probably would have lost and that would have burst his balloon of omnipotence, but because he would have forced his fellow Alabamians to choose between their two heroes who didn't pussyfoot around against the Yankees.

Besides, The Bear doesn't properly belong in that line. Successful Southern politicians are pugnacious, like Wallace, perhaps mean, irascible at best. Southern generals, by contrast, are courtly and noble, permitting their troops to do the necessary bloodletting—within the rules, of course. The Bear is a general, and it is important to the state that he win his battles honorably. It is all the more significant that, during his time in the wilderness, The Bear admits to having cheated, to having wallowed in expedience; that it was only his conjoining again with Alabama that made him whole and pure once more. And what a union it has been! . . .

RIDING HIGH in 1961 with the first of his six national championships, Bear was borne aloft after the Tide rolled Auburn 34–0.

MARVIN E. NEWMAN

1940 | TOM HARMON, Michigan's Old 98, was easy to recognize as he powered his way to the Heisman in
his school's signature leather helmet, which later landed in the Hall of Fame. | *Photograph by* ALFRED EISENSTAEDT

1958 | FLYING BRUINS converged on a loose ball during UCLA's 20–17 loss to Rose Bowl–bound Cal. | *Photograph by* JOHN G. ZIMMERMAN

> THE ALL-DECADE TEAM

FIRST TEAM		SECOND TEAM	
E	**Tack Hardwick** HARVARD	E	**Guy Chamberlain** NEBRASKA WESLEYAN, NEBRASKA
E	**Frank Hinkey** YALE	E	**Paul Robeson** RUTGERS
T	**Wilbur Henry** WASHINGTON & JEFFERSON	T	**Marshall Newell** HARVARD
T	**Belf West** COLGATE	T	**Josh Cody** VANDERBILT
G	**Pudge Heffelfinger** YALE	G	**Stan Pennock** HARVARD
G	**Truxton Hare** PENN	G	**Joe Alexander** SYRACUSE
C	**Bob Peck** PITTSBURGH	C	**Germany Schulz** MICHIGAN
B	**Jim Thorpe** CARLISLE	B	**Edgar Allan Poe** PRINCETON
B	**Walter Eckersall** CHICAGO	B	**Elmer Oliphant** PURDUE, ARMY
B	**Ted Coy** YALE	B	**Fritz Pollard** BROWN
B	**Willie Heston** SAN JOSE STATE, MICHIGAN	B	**Chic Harley** OHIO STATE

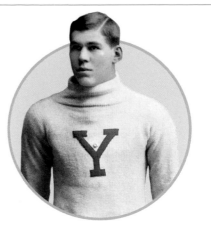

> NICKNAMES <

William [Pudge] Heffelfinger ∧
Earl [Tuffy] Abell
Frank [The Iron Major] Cavanaugh
Raymond [Snooks] Dowd
[Gloomy] Gil Dobie
Paddy [The Wasp] Driscoll
Charlie [The Miracle Man] Gelbert
George [The Gipper] Gipp
Huntington [Tack] Hardwick
Charles [Chic] Harley
Wilbur [Fats] Henry
Lou [Luigi Piccolo] Little
Bob [Tiny] Maxwell
Gene [The Meteoric Midget] Miller
Alfred Earle [Greasy] Neale
Stan [Bags] Pennock
Frederick [Fritz] Pollard
Adolph [Germany] Schulz
Ed [Brick] Travis
Glenn [Pop] Warner
Fielding [Hurry Up] Yost

NATIONAL CHAMPION, COACH

1890 **HARVARD** ... George Stewart, George Adams	1900 **YALE** .... Malcolm McBride	1910 **HARVARD** .... Percy Haughton
1891 **YALE** .... Walter Camp	1901 **MICHIGAN** .... Fielding Yost	1911 **PRINCETON** .... Bill Roper
1892 **YALE** .... Walter Camp	1902 **MICHIGAN** .... Fielding Yost	1912 **HARVARD** .... Percy Haughton
1893 **PRINCETON** .... Tom Trenchard	1903 **PRINCETON** .... Hart Hillebrand	1913 **HARVARD** .... Percy Haughton
1894 **YALE** .... William Rhodes	1904 **PENN** .... Carl Williams	1914 **ARMY** .... Charley Daly
1895 **PENN** .... George Woodruff	1905 **CHICAGO** .... Amos Alonzo Stagg	1915 **CORNELL** .... Al Sharpe
1896 **PRINCETON** .... Garrett Cochran	1906 **PRINCETON** .... Bill Roper	1916 **PITT** .... Pop Warner
1897 **PENN** .... George Woodruff	1907 **YALE** .... Bill Knox	1917 **GEORGIA TECH** .... John Heisman
1898 **HARVARD** .... W. Cameron Forbes	1908 **PENN** .... Sol Metzger	1918 **PITT** .... Pop Warner
1899 **HARVARD** .... Benjamin Diblee	1909 **YALE** .... Howard Jones	1919 **HARVARD** .... Bob Fisher

>> DYNASTIES OF THE EARLY ERA

Yale

New Haven was the hothouse of football, home to such seminal figures as Walter Camp, Amos Alonzo Stagg and Pudge Heffelfinger. In 47 seasons from 1872 to 1919, the Elis were judged the national champion 11 times—the same number of seasons in which the Elis' opponents were all held scoreless.

Notre Dame

By pioneering the forward pass and building a myth around doomed triple-threat star George Gipp, the formidable Fighting Irish became the nation's most popular team. The game's most hallowed figure, Knute Rockne, arrived first as an ace receiver, then (starting in 1918) as coach.

Princeton beat Syracuse 12–9 on Oct. 10, 1914, two weeks before the Tigers (with ball) opened Palmer Stadium, their home for 82 years.

Princeton v

After a defeat by Rutgers in the first college football game, in 1869, the Tigers went 59 years without a losing season, going unbeaten 21 times and winning seven national titles. All-Americas included Edgar Allan Poe, Philip King, Langdon Lea and Arthur Wheeler.

Harvard

The Crimson won seven national titles from 1890 to 1919 and went 71-7-5 under innovative coach Percy Haughton. The finest player from that era was dropkicking whiz Charlie Brickley '15, who remained Harvard's career scoring leader until 2006.

Michigan

Fielding Yost's "Point-Per-Minute" Wolverines, featuring back Willie Heston, were a powerhouse at the turn of the century, winning or sharing national titles from 1901 to '04 while going 43-0-1 and outscoring opponents 2,326 to 34.

> EPIC GAMES

< Cumberland *vs.* Georgia Tech

October 7, 1916

The first quarter ended 63–0, the second 126–0. Coach John Heisman's Yellow Jackets did not throw a single pass and neither team made a first down all game. Cumberland fumbled nine times; Tech's Jim Preas was 18 for 18 on conversions. The final score: Georgia Tech 222, Cumberland 0—still records for total points and margin of victory in a college game.

Notre Dame *vs.* Army

November 1, 1913

After having scant success going through Army's rock-solid line in the first quarter, the visiting Irish decided to go over it: Gus Dorais threw the ball repeatedly to Joe Pliska and Knute Rockne, completing an astounding 13 of 17 passes for 243 yards, shocking the Cadets 35–13 and ushering in a new era of offensive football.

Carlisle *vs.* Army

November 9, 1912

To take full advantage of Jim Thorpe's running, passing and punting prowess, Carlisle coach Pop Warner had devised a formation called the single wing. Army's fabled defense, which included a cadet named Dwight Eisenhower, keyed on Thorpe, but he still sprinted for a 97-yard touchdown as the underdog Indians thrashed the Cadets 27–6.

> CAMPUS CULTURE

YOU'VE GOT TO . . .

READ IT: *The Red Badge of Courage*, Stephen Crane; *Adventures of Huckleberry Finn*, Mark Twain; *The Jungle*, Upton Sinclair; *The Hound of the Baskervilles*, Sir Arthur Conan Doyle; *Winesburg, Ohio*, Sherwood Anderson; *Dracula*, Bram Stoker; *Around the World in 80 Days*, Jules Verne; *Alice's Adventures in Wonderland*, Lewis Carroll; Frank Merriwell stories, Burt L. Standish

SEE IT: Ziegfeld Follies, *The Nickelodeon*, *Birth of a Nation*, *The Floorwalker*, *Daddy-Long-Legs*, Keystone Cops, Buffalo Bill Cody's Wild West show, W.C. Fields and Jack Benny on the vaudeville circuit

Push ball (at Columbia in 1910) was the perfect recreation for an innocent time.

"The credit belongs to the man who is actually in the arena, whose face is marred by dust and sweat and blood."

—*Theodore Roosevelt, at the Sorbonne, April 23, 1910*

HEAR IT: Scott Joplin, W. C. Handy, Eubie Blake, Al Jolson, Irving Berlin

DISCUSS IT: Immigration, the Wright Brothers, Panama Canal, temperance, relativity, women's suffrage, Jack Johnson, transcontinental railroad, periodic table, horseless carriages, Gibson Girls

DEAL WITH IT: The Great War, influenza, robber barons, Bolsheviks, the *Titanic*, Krakatoa, Jim Crow

HAVE IT: Victrola, electric lights, telephone, Sears, Roebuck catalogue, canned food, peanut butter, Coca-Cola

WEAR IT: Straw boaters, spats, striped blazers, starched shirts, top hats, high-buttoned shoes, corsets

DO IT: Ping-Pong, fox-trot, tennis, penny-arcade games

> SMARTEST GUY IN THE WORLD

THOMAS EDISON
America's most prolific inventor, his creations (incandescent lightbulb, phonograph, motion picture camera) and perfection of others' work (typewriter, stock ticker) resulted in 1,093 patents.

> BY THE NUMBERS

25 | Players per side in the first college football game, between Rutgers and Princeton on Nov. 6, 1869.

63 | Consecutive games without a loss for Washington from 1907 through '17, an alltime record.

11 | Years (from 1860 to '71) that football was banned on the Harvard campus after school officials deemed it too rough.

77 | Years after graduation that Rutgers end Paul Robeson was inducted into the College Football Hall of Fame. Robeson, All-America in 1917 and '18 and later a singing and acting star, was shunned over his refusal to denounce communism.

18 | Estimated football fatalities in 1905 (three of them college players), leading to rules changes, including legalization of the forward pass.

35 | Consecutive games, from 1890 to '93, in which Yale held opponents scoreless, a record.

140 × 70 | The original dimensions, in yards, of a football field.

INNOVATOR

Walter Camp
"The Father of American Football" was no misnomer for the Yale icon: Camp was integral in conceiving the scrimmage line, snap, downs, arrangement of players, scoring systems—and the All-America team.

2005 | A HEADS-UP play by Alabama's Wallace Gilberry (92) on South Carolina's
William Brown got the attention of a hatless Mark Anderson. | *Photograph by* BRANTLEY HARELSON

1989 | MEMBERS OF the Texas A&M honor guard were clearly behind their Aggies when they butted heads with bitter rival Texas. | *Photograph by* RICH CLARKSON

1962 | YOUNG MISSES from Ole Miss showed their colors at the Cotton Bowl before their Rebels fell to Texas 12–7. | *Photograph by* HY PESKIN

ABSOLUTE ZERO

BY WILLIAM NACK

During the 1939 regular season, Tennessee faced 10 foes, and not one of them scored a point.

—*from* SI, DECEMBER 28, 1998 – JANUARY 4, 1999

ALABAMA SAFETY HERSHEL Mosley looked upfield, at all those 'Bama bodies felled and piled like cordwood in the late-October light, and figured he might end up the only defender standing. In the middle of the field, with his own goal line 30 yards behind him, he set himself and thought, What do I do? He sensed he dare not move.

Johnny Butler was coming straight at him, the football cradled in his left arm, and for a moment there during the second quarter at Shields-Watkins Field in Knoxville—before more than 40,000 throaty souls, then the largest crowd ever to have attended a sporting event in Tennessee—Butler looked like Casper in cleats: "a dancing, dodging, untacklable ghost," as Grantland Rice would describe him the next day.

Mosley watched Butler's run unfold before him. "It was like poetry," he says now, some 60 years later. "It looked like it had been choreographed." Indeed, by this afternoon of Oct. 21, 1939, much of what the Volunteers had done of late, on both sides of the line, had seemed flawlessly scripted. They hadn't lost a game since Nov. 13, 1937, when Vanderbilt had beaten them 13–7. They had won their last 16 games in a row, a streak that embraced the entire '38 season, in which Tennessee had gone 11–0, beaten Oklahoma 17–0 in the Orange Bowl and shared the national championship with Texas Christian.

By the 1939 game against Alabama, the Vols were also on their way to setting two NCAA records that may never be broken: They would hold their opponents scoreless through 17 straight regular-season games and 71 consecutive quarters, from the second quarter of the game against LSU on Oct. 29, 1938, to the first quarter of the game against the Crimson Tide on Oct. 19, 1940. Tennessee was also in the midst of what could turn out to be the last unflawed regular season in college football, a campaign in which the Vols went undefeated, untied and unscored upon. They won their 10 regular season games in '39 by a combined score of 212–0.

Of all that these Volunteers are remembered for, however, nothing remotely approaches the drama that ensued on Oct. 21 when the 5' 10", 160-pound Butler, playing tailback in Tennessee's single-wing offense, took the snap from Norbert Ackerman on the Tennessee 44-yard line. Butler crossed the 50, cut suddenly right and raced across the field to the other sideline, the hands of Tide defenders grabbing at him as he went. There was Mosley, awaiting him near the 30. Butler sprinted straight at him, faked right, cut left. "I leaned, and the little pissant cut back right again!" Mosley says. "He cut twice on me! Fooled me."

Butler blew past Mosley, and as he got to the 20, he danced in front of defensive back Jimmy Nelson until blocking back Ike Peel reappeared and cut Nelson down. Loose at last, Butler raced the final 20 yards to score and put the Vols ahead 6–0. It was officially a 56-yard gallop, but most observers believe Butler went at least twice that far.

The demoralized Tide never got into the game, which Tennessee won 21–0. Not only had Butler instantly entered the pantheon of Volunteers football but he had also done so against the Vols' bitterest rival in the most ballyhooed game of the year. In fact, of all the games Tennessee won during its extraordinary run, none did more to commend it to history than the 1939 victory over Alabama. The Volunteers had four All-Americas that year: tailback George (Bad News) Cafego and guards Ed Molinsky and Bob Suffridge, all three of whom are in the College Football Hall of Fame, and tackle Abe Shires. Tennessee also had unheralded 187-pound fullback-linebacker Len Coffman, regarded by surviving members of the team as its finest player, pound for pound. "I don't believe I ever saw a better team in my entire coaching and playing career," venerable Pitt coach Jock Sutherland told Rice. "A team magnificently coached and drilled."

The architect of this precision drill was Tennessee's legendary coach, Robert Neyland, a West Point graduate who ran his offense like the First Engineers major that he'd been in World War I. He was an innovative master—he was the first coach, for instance, to use film to evaluate games—and he was more comfortable without the ball. Neyland had seven maxims, the first of which was, "The team that makes the fewest mistakes will win." During his 21 years at Tennessee he coached 216 games, and in nearly half of them (106) the Vols' opponents didn't score. "If he had 10 points on you," end Ed Cifers says, "he'd quick-kick on first down just to give you the ball back, hoping you would make a mistake." . . .

ROUGH AND READY, Len Coffman headed off LSU's Charles Anastasio (46) during a 1939 whitewash that showcased the Volunteers' unyielding style.

1962 | THE ELVIS of college football, Alabama's Joe Namath wowed coeds and coach Bear Bryant with his passes during the Tide's 10–1 season. | *Photograph by* NEIL LEIFER

1971 | HEISMAN WINNER Jim Plunkett gunned Stanford to a Rose Bowl upset of previously unbeaten Ohio State. | *Photograph by* SHEEDY & LONG

1941 | THE FIRST penalty marker, sewn from pieces of a Halloween costume, was used in a Youngstown–Oklahoma City game. | *Photograph by* DAVID BERKWITZ

1998 | A FLAG flew when contact with Air Force's Dylan Newman by a BYU defensive back prompted an interference call. | *Photograph by* ROBERT BECK

COLLEGE FOOTBALL HALL OF FAME

45

2002 | DELIRIOUS CAL fans ran a post pattern after their Golden Bears thrashed Stanford 30–7 in the 105th renewal of the Big Game. | *Photograph by* DONALD MIRALLE

1957 | ARRAYED IN scarlet and white, sun-splashed Ohio State boosters radiated joy as their national champion Buckeyes edged Iowa 17–13. | *Photograph by* JERRY COOKE

LIKE A BOLT OF LIGHTNING

BY DAN JENKINS

Nebraska's juggernaut of the early '70s had many weapons in its arsenal, but none more potent than the electrifying Johnny Rodgers. —*from* SI, NOVEMBER 13, 1972

IT WOULD NOT BE FAIR TO THE legends of all the Red Granges, Tom Harmons, Doak Walkers and O.J. Simpsons to say that Johnny Rodgers might be the most excruciatingly exciting player who ever made forced landings on real grass or artificial turf, but he is surely among the all-timers in the category of jerking the occupants of entire stadiums upward every time he touches the ball. Or, for that matter, of causing a whole defense to feel like it was coming down with a head cold if he even goes in motion before the snap.

For his size, which is no more than 5' 9" and 173 pounds, Rodgers has to be the most devastating player who ever suited up, and every Saturday he manages to invent a new repertoire of dance steps with the ball that leaves national TV audiences and his own hoarse following mercilessly agog at the wonder of it all.

Last Saturday, on a glorious day in the Rockies, he was doing it all again against a rugged physical team, Colorado, that was aching for a shot at him. With a little help from his friends, Rodgers simply destroyed Colorado with a spectacular display of all his talent, which is known statistically around the NCAA records bureau as All-Purpose Running. Basically, that means returning kicks and interceptions and catching passes with some occasional rushing from scrimmage. Rodgers all-purposed Colorado for 266 yards, most of it on punt returns, and Nebraska looked as strong as it ever has, winning 33–10.

About every 10 minutes throughout the afternoon Colorado would kick the ball to Rodgers for some mysterious reason, and here he'd come, a fiery little figure of bounding, blurring, flitting energy. Nobody has ever stopped and started as quickly or retained his balance so beautifully in so many awkward positions. Colorado punted to him six times and kicked off to him once, and every time he stood under the football the thought must have occurred to all of the 52,128 people in the stadium that this might be a Nebraska touchdown.

Rodgers never went all the way with a kick, but he did go immense distances, such as 59 yards (partly nullified by a clip), 40 yards, 38 yards, 26 yards and 22 yards, and a couple of the runs just were not to be believed as he darted, retreated, sidestepped and spun his way over the yardage stripes like a Ping-Pong ball that somebody had let loose in a wind tunnel.

And the thing about it is, it has become routine. He has been doing it for 33 games in the Nebraska uniform, all this returning, receiving and reversing, and no wonder Bob Devaney wants to retire from coaching after this season. Rodgers will be gone, much to the delight of the rest of the Big Eight.

He has three more regular-season games to play for the Cornhuskers, however, and undoubtedly a bowl game after that before his brilliant collegiate career will have ended. But even when his final statistics are totaled up and enshrined somewhere around Lincoln, they can hardly be much more impressive than they already are. Dwell on these numbers, if you will: In three seasons, or 33 games through last week, Rodgers has returned 99 punts for 1,564 yards; he has returned 33 kickoffs for 790 yards; he has caught 134 passes for 2,488 yards; he has rushed 124 times for another 688 yards, 5,530 yards in all, and he has scored 42 touchdowns.

In Rodgers's case, though, statistics are inadequate. Figures don't reveal anything about how thunderous the Nebraska attack has been for three years in other departments just because of his presence in the lineup. As a pro scout said, "Everywhere they put him—at slot, wing, flanker, anywhere—you can see the defense lean a little."

And the figures don't describe all the astonishing thrills provided by a player who has that knack of making a mere six-yard run seem like a journey into outer space.

But they probably ought to be recited here and now, because that funny old thing called the Heisman Trophy ballot will be going into the mails soon, and if Johnny Rodgers is not this season's leading candidate (if not, in fact, the only candidate) then most of the voters must be planning on writing in the names of their cousins. . . .

THE ELUSIVE Rodgers was credited with 5,586 all-purpose yards (then a record), but probably covered twice that much ground while dodging defenders.

1963 | SEEKING AN overview, Navy quarterback Roger Staubach hopped to it in front of his fellow Midshipmen and coach Wayne Hardin. | *Photograph by* NEIL LEIFER

1964 | TOP-RANKED Texas and coach Darrell Royal had their game faces on before their 28–6 Cotton Bowl dismantling of No. 2 Navy. | *Photograph by* NEIL LEIFER

1974 | IT WAS a real bodice ripper when quarterback Richard Todd and Alabama scrambled to a 17–13 win over archrival Auburn. | *Photograph by* NEIL LEIFER

1993 | FLORIDA'S D was not as elastic as it might've seemed when Georgia's David Weeks (55) grabbed Florida's Matt Pearson from behind. | *Photograph by* BILL FRAKES

NO CONTEST

BY RICK REILLY

The NFL has its vast legions of devoted fans, but let us count the ways in which the collegiate game will always be superior.

—*from* SI, FALL 1995

ANYBODY WHO HAS NOT HAD large portions of his cerebellum removed for scientific purposes knows that college football is better than pro football the way that Sean Connery is better than Roger Moore. Still, it's always nice to remind ourselves why. ❧ For one thing, college football has Ralphie, Uga and Smokey the Blue Tick Coon Hound. Pro football has Crazy George on too many Jolt Colas.

College football has picnic blankets with candelabras at Harvard-Yale, brats on the grill at Michigan–Ohio State, cold beers at the Esso Club gas pumps before Clemson home games. Pro football has stadium nachos—now with actual foodlike cheese substance!

College football has Auburn's *Tiger Talk* radio show with Terry Bowden and calls like the following one:

"Coach Bowden?"

"Yessir."

"This is Bobby Dan Tallbutt down in Huntsville."

"Yessir, Bobby Dan."

"Just wanted to say War Eagle."

"War Eagle, Bobby Dan."

Pro football, meanwhile, has 103-FM's 24-hour *Sports Zoo*, in which Mad Mike continually screams things to the Captain, such as: "It's time the truth was told!!!!! Gale Sayers sucked!!!!!"

College football has rich traditions: walking the Grove at Ole Miss, standing up for A&M, dotting the *i* at Ohio State. Pro football, on the other hand, has rich marketing guys with not enough to do. If pro football had its way, we would have AT&T Presents the i Plan: dotting the *i* with today's guest dotter—Willard Scott!

College football has *The Notre Dame Victory March, On Wisconsin, Hail to the Victors.* Pro football has *Houston Oilers No. 1*, which goes:

Houston Oilers, Houston Oilers

College football has rivalries that have not changed in 50 years: Army-Navy, Texas-Oklahoma, Stanford-Cal, Florida-Georgia and about 25 others that keep players awake all night and cause receptionists to answer phones by saying, "Beat Texas, Monolith Oil, how can I help you?" Pro football hasn't had a decent rivalry since Johnson-Goldwater.

College football is the bonfires at Texas A&M, between the hedges at Georgia, up on Rocky Top at Tennessee. Pro football is performance-weighted draft picks offsetting a free-agent sell-off to skirt the salary cap.

College football has Hook 'em, Horns! Whoo, pig, sooey! Roll, Tide! Pro football has giant clapping hands on the scoreboard, dot races and Chinstrap Nights.

College football has Athens, Ga.; Eugene, Ore.; and Madison, Wis. Pro football has not one but two teams in East Rutherford, N.J.

College football is an Ohio State helmet adorned with Buckeyes, a Florida State helmet adorned with hatchets, a Penn State helmet adorned with nothing. Pro football is basically a whole lot of black and teal now, though some teams are trying something vastly different and refreshing: teal and black.

In college football, nobody is a free agent. Nobody gets traded. Nobody sits out his option year. In pro football this off-season, more than 200 players changed teams. What you're basically doing is rooting for your team's uniform design against the other team's uniform design.

College football is yell practice. Point push-ups. Shining the helmets. Pro football is the Buffalo Bills' professional cheerleaders, the Buffalo Jills, who recently formed a union.

College football is LSU's Tiger Stadium at night. Spring football in Strawberry Canyon at Cal. Annapolis when the leaves turn. Pro football is a guy with sleet hanging off his hat outside the Pontiac Silverdome, trying to get his butterfly valve unstuck.

College football is the Southern University Jaguar Band halftime show, runny makeup on homecoming queens, a 92-year-old halfback at midfield. Pro football is a halftime show with Michael Jackson attempting a groin pull.

College football has Keith Jackson saying, "Whoa, Nellie, we're fixin' to have a barn burner!" Pro football has Beasley Reece and Jerry Glanville discussing the roll-up zone.

A college football player will tell you he loves his team, will play there for four years and will wear his school ring the rest of his life. A pro football player will tell you he loves his team, will play there for six months, sign with a team in the same division, play for six other teams before his career is over—and wear his school ring the rest of his life . . . .

THE COLLEGE game stokes passions that money can't buy, as Billy Kinard and his cheerleading bride showed after Ole Miss's win over TCU in the '56 Cotton Bowl.

1991 | N.C. STATE'S Charles Davenport (in red) drew a bead on a pass lofted over Georgia Tech defender Tom Johnson. | *Photograph by* AL TIELEMANS

2006 | NOTRE DAME wideout David Grimes (11) and Michigan cornerback Leon Hall flat-out pursued the same objective. | *Photograph by* MICHAEL CONROY

THE 1920s

> THE ALL-DECADE TEAM

FIRST TEAM		SECOND TEAM	
E	Bennie Oosterbaan MICHIGAN	E	Wes Fesler OHIO STATE
E	Brick Muller CAL	E	Joe Donchess PITTSBURGH
T	Bronko Nagurski MINNESOTA	T	Century Milstead WABASH, YALE
T	Ed Weir NEBRASKA	T	Stan Keck PRINCETON
G	Carl Diehl DARTMOUTH	G	Charles Hubbard HARVARD
G	Jack Cannon NOTRE DAME	G	Ed Hess OHIO STATE
C	Mel Hein WASHINGTON STATE	C	Ben Ticknor HARVARD
B	George Gipp NOTRE DAME	B	Frank Carideo NOTRE DAME
B	Red Grange ILLINOIS	B	Tom Davies PITTSBURGH
B	Ernie Nevers STANFORD	B	Benny Friedman MICHIGAN
B	Chris Cagle SW LOUISIANA, ARMY	B	George Wilson WASHINGTON

>NICKNAMES<

Bronislau [Bronko] Nagurski ∧
Heartley [Hunk] Anderson
Ralph [Moon] Baker
Harry [Blond Beast] Baujan
Jim [Wichita Whiz] Bausch
[Sleepy] Jim Crowley
Red [The Galloping Ghost] Grange
Edwin [Goat] Hale
Homer [Pop] Hazel
Mel [Old Indestructible] Hein
Gordon [Sherlock] Holmes
Mort [Devil May] Kaer
Ray [Rags] Matthews
Jack [Spindle Legs] McDowall
Gene [Wild Bull] McEver
Johnny [Blood] McNally
Don [Midnight] Miller
Ernie [Big Dog] Nevers
Ed [Cannonball] Tryon
Francis [Close the Gates of Mercy] Schmidt
Herb [Cobblcs] Sturhahn

NATIONAL CHAMPION, COACH

'20	CAL	Andy Smith
'21	CORNELL	Gil Dobie
'22	CORNELL	Gil Dobie
'23	ILLINOIS	Bob Zuppke
'24	NOTRE DAME	Knute Rockne
'25	ALABAMA, DARTMOUTH	<Wallace Wade, Jesse Hawley
'26	ALABAMA, STANFORD	Wallace Wade, Pop Warner >
'27	ILLINOIS	Bob Zuppke
'28	GEORGIA TECH	Bill Alexander
'29	NOTRE DAME	Knute Rockne

>> THE DECADE'S DYNASTIES

Cal
How dominant were Andy Smith's "Wonder Teams?" They didn't suffer their first loss of the decade until 1925, going 46-0-4 and making three trips to the Rose Bowl. The big man at Berkeley was end Brick Muller, a two-time All-America.

Notre Dame >
For the decade Knute Rockne's Fighting Irish went an unholy 83-11-3, parlaying undefeated seasons into national titles in 1924 and '29 while enlarging a national following. Rockne's genius was apparent in his preference for smaller but speedier players, best exemplified by the '24 team's storied Four Horsemen backfield.

Illinois
The Illini featured arguably the game's greatest player, headline-making halfback Red Grange—the Galloping Ghost. Grange was key in winning the 1923 national title, but after he left, coach Bob Zuppke snared another in '27.

Alabama
The Crimson Tide's undefeated 1925 national champions allowed one touchdown in nine regular-season games and, behind halfback Johnny Mack Brown, put Southern football on the map by beating heavily favored Washington in the Rose Bowl. Wallace Wade's boys repeated in '26, with another national title.

Cornell
"Gloomy Gil" Dobie's Big Red went 8–0 each season from 1921 through '23. Two captains, quarterback George Pfann and halfback Eddie Kaw, led the two-time national champs.

Marty Brill was one of the backs who helped Notre Dame stiff-arm its opposition.

> EPIC GAMES

<Michigan *vs.* Illinois
October 18, 1924

Red Grange *(left)* dedicated Illinois's new Memorial Stadium by running six times for 265 yards and four TDs in the first 12 minutes of Illinois's 39–14 win. The Galloping Ghost finished with 402 yards and six TDs, which legendary coach Amos Alonzo Stagg called "the most spectacular single-handed performance ever delivered in a major game."

Army *vs.* Notre Dame
October 18, 1924

A crowd of 55,000 jammed the Polo Grounds for a matchup of two renowned programs. The Irish, powered by speedy backs Harry Stuhldreher, Jim Crowley, Don Miller and Elmer Layden, beat the Cadets 13–7, prompting writer Grantland Rice to dub them "The Four Horsemen," which helped make them the most famous backfield in football history.

Georgia Tech *vs.* Cal
January 1, 1929 • ROSE BOWL

Having outscored opponents by an average of 19.2 points, Tech was considered the nation's top team but might've fallen had the Bears' Roy Riegels not returned a second-quarter Tech fumble to his own end zone. The resulting safety accounted for the winning margin in the Yellow Jackets' 8–7 win and earned Riegels the nickname "Wrong Way."

> CAMPUS CULTURE

YOU'VE GOT TO . . .

READ IT: *The Great Gatsby*, F. Scott Fitzgerald; *The Sun Also Rises*, Ernest Hemingway; *All Quiet on the Western Front*, Erich Maria Remarque; *The Waste Land*, T.S. Eliot; *Babbitt*, Sinclair Lewis; *The Sound and the Fury*, William Faulkner; *Lady Chatterley's Lover*, D.H. Lawrence

HEAR IT: Louis Armstrong, Duke Ellington, Bix Beiderbecke, Al Jolson, Bessie Smith, Rudy Vallee, Rodgers and Hart, Hoagy Carmichael, Blind Lemon Jefferson, Fanny Brice, Blind Willie McTell, Amos 'n' Andy

> "The chief business of the American people is business. They are profoundly concerned with buying, selling, investing and prospering in the world."

—President Calvin Coolidge, to the American Society of Newspaper Editors, Washington, D.C., Jan. 25, 1925

SEE IT: *The Jazz Singer*, Harold Lloyd and Charlie Chaplin comedies, Tom Mix westerns, *The Mark of Zorro*, *The Phantom of the Opera*, *The Hunchback of Notre Dame*, *The Sheik*, *The Virginian*

DISCUSS IT: Harlem renaissance, Miss America Pageant, Babe Ruth, King Tut's tomb, League of Nations, Charles Lindbergh, the Scopes monkey trial, Fatty Arbuckle

The infant medium of radio allowed students to broadcast on campus and to dial in distant voices.

DEAL WITH IT: Stock market crash, the Black Sox, Prohibition, Al Capone, Ku Klux Klan, communism

HAVE IT: The vote (women), bootleg liquor, crystal radio, Model T, PEZ, phonograph records

WEAR IT: Raccoon coat, flapper's cloche hat and short skirt, mail-order suits, bow tie, English driving cap, garters, linen knickers

DO IT: The Charleston, crossword puzzles, dance marathons, flagpole sitting

> SMARTEST GUY IN THE WORLD

SIGMUND FREUD
With his groundbreaking theories of human behavior that particularly emphasized the importance of the unconscious mind, this Viennese physician radically transformed everyday life and especially sexuality.

> BY THE NUMBERS

0 | Total points by Cal and Washington & Jefferson in the only scoreless Rose Bowl, in 1922.

8 | Years after the 1920 death of star back George Gipp that Notre Dame coach Knute Rockne delivered his "Win one for the Gipper" speech, before his team upset Army 12–6.

5 | Passes intercepted in 1929 by Arkansas's Wear Schoonover, the Southwest Conference's first All-America, during a 13–2 win over Centenary.

32 | Fumbles by Iowa and Wisconsin in a game on Nov. 7, 1925, played during a driving snowstorm in Iowa City.

2 | Seasons (1925 and '26) that tackle Marion Morrison, later known as John Wayne, played at USC.

8 | Seasons played by Chris (Red) Cagle: four each at Southwestern Louisiana and Army, where he was a three-time All-America from 1927 to '29.

10 | Yards the unpadded goal posts were pushed back from the goal line in 1927 to limit injuries to players.

INNOVATOR
Bob Zuppke
Much more than Red Grange's coach at Illinois, Zuppke popularized the huddle, concocted the screen pass and the flea-flicker—and sought to limit injuries by designing a helmet with improved shock-absorbing properties.

2007 | A BEAR among Ducks, Justin Forsett broke loose for 101 rushing yards and two touchdowns in Cal's 31–24 win at Oregon. | *Photograph by* PETER READ MILLER

1975 | USC QUARTERBACK and future Rhodes Scholar Pat Haden smartly directed the Trojans to a Rose Bowl upset of Ohio State. | *Photograph by* RICH CLARKSON

1959 | SPRUNG BY Emile Fournet (65) and his other blockers, LSU's Billy Cannon (20) headed upfield against Baylor on his way to the Heisman. | *Photograph by* BETTMANN/CORBIS

2005 | GRAMBLING FELL to Washington State 48–7, but the marching Tigers kept the battle of the bands much more competitive. | *Photograph by* JESSE BEALS

2004 | EYES RIGHT, the Florida A & M band's drum majors commanded attention at halftime when the Rattlers visited Temple. | *Photograph by* MICHAEL SUGRUE

A SPECIAL KIND OF BRUTE

BY DAN JENKINS

For Dick Butkus the good life at Illinois consisted mainly of picking apart blockers and punishing the guy with the ball.
—from SI, OCTOBER 12, 1964

IF EVERY COLLEGE FOOTBALL TEAM had a linebacker like Dick Butkus, all fullbacks would soon be three feet tall and sing soprano. Dick Butkus is a special kind of brute whose particular talent is mashing runners into curious shapes. He is, in fact, the product of an era—an era that has seen his position properly glamorized by such professional primates as Sam Huff and Joe Schmidt, and an era that has fostered defensive specialists in college through the gradual easing up of substitution rules. But while the 1964 season has therefore uncaged a rare group of first-rate collegiate linebackers, there is only one Dick Butkus. No linebacker mashes as many opponents as this Illinois senior, and what is more he does it in the Big Ten, a conference that offers little else to mash except fellow brutes.

There are a lot of reasons why Butkus is the most destructive defensive player in collegiate football, one who personally made 145 tackles and caused 10 fumbles last season and who this season has a good chance to become the first lineman in 15 years to win the Heisman Trophy.

The first reason is his size. Butkus is 6' 3" and weighs 243 pounds, which means that he is the biggest college linebacker on a list of exceptionally good ones that includes Texas's Tommy Nobis, Washington's Rick Redman, Auburn's Bill Cody, Duke's Mike Curtis, Arkansas' Ronnie Caveness, Georgia Tech's Dave Simmons and Rice's Malcolm Walker. While these players are just as tough and willing as Butkus, they cannot hit as hard because they simply are not as big. Butkus not only hits, he crushes and squeezes opponents with thick arms that also are extremely long. At any starting point on his build, he is big, well-proportioned and getting bigger. Once this summer Butkus reached a hard 268 pounds, but he trimmed some of it off for fear of losing speed.

There are, to be sure, linebackers who are faster and quicker than Butkus—Texas's Nobis, for example, is perhaps the quickest of all—but none of them have Butkus' instinct for getting to the play.

"He has intuition," says Illinois coach Pete Elliott, whose sudden success last year is traceable in part to the day he recruited Butkus. "On the first play of his first spring practice, before we had told him anything, he smelled out a screen pass and broke it up. In two seasons Dick has only been out of one screen pass. By that I mean [on all others] he either diagnosed them and forced an incompletion or got there and made the tackle."

Elliott says, "He's naturally great at jamming up the middle against running plays, but somehow he manages to cover wide real good. He gets there, you know, because he wants to. Football is everything to him. When we have a workout canceled because of bad weather or something, he gets angry, almost despondent. He lives for contact."

Contact to Butkus is really only one thing: the moment of impact with the player unfortunate enough to have the ball. All of that other business, such as people bumping into him, foolishly trying to block him, he ignores. He is hurrying to the fun which, he says, consists of "getting a good measure on a guy and stripping him down."

Butkus first began taking it out of opposing players as an All-America prep-school fullback at Chicago Vocational High. Even then he preferred defense and made 70% of his team's tackles. As a member of a full-blooded Lithuanian family of nine, growing up in a blue-collar district of Chicago's South Side, Butkus had never known many sports other than football. He used to swim some and he tried baseball, but from the eighth grade on football was it. And Big Ten football was what he always looked forward to.

"I had a lot of offers," he says, inoffensively. "But I didn't never really consider any of 'em except Illinois. Northwestern was . . . well, they ain't my kind of people. Notre Dame looked too hard."

With casual honesty Butkus admits he is no honor student. "If I was smart enough to be a doctor, I'd be a doctor," he shrugs. "I ain't, so I'm a football player." . . .

BORN TO hammer ballcarriers, Butkus (50) set such a high standard for the Illini that the annual award for the top college linebacker is named after him.

1970 | LINED UP to defend their national championship, the Texas Longhorns offensive starters were arrayed in their Eye-formation. | *Photograph by* NEIL LEIFER

1999 | FEW WERE able to lay a hand on future Heisman-winning quarterback Eric Crouch and Nebraska during their 12–1 season. | *Photograph by* PETER READ MILLER

1967 | PLAYING BATMAN, Tennessee's Jimmy Weatherford knocked down the pass and Alabama's Dennis Homan in a 24–13 Vols victory. | *Photograph by* WALTER IOOSS JR.

1988 | FINGERTIP CONTROL enabled Oklahoma State All-America Hart Lee Dykes to stretch the D and make one of 203 career catches. | *Photograph by* JOHN BIEVER

1986 | WILD CHILD of the Sooners, linebacker Brian Bosworth was not just attitude, earning the Butkus Award for his eye-catching play at Oklahoma. | *Photograph by* JOHN BIEVER

1935 | AS A member of Fordham's vaunted Seven Blocks of Granite, right guard Vince Lombardi (opposite) laid the foundation that would make him the NFL's most iconic coach. | *Photograph by* AP

2002 | GEORGIA'S BELOVED Uga IV kept his cool during the Bulldogs' hotly contested 27–25 win over Alabama. | *Photograph by* GARY BOGDON

2000 | THE CITADEL'S Corey White (left) and Aaron Capps found cold comfort on a steamy preseason media day in South Carolina. | *Photograph by* ALAN HAWES

THE GOLDEN BOYS

BY PAUL ZIMMERMAN

After World War II, Notre Dame fielded the greatest college football team in history, but which unbeaten Irish juggernaut was it: the '46 or the '47 squad? —*from* SI, NOVEMBER 24, 1997

I MET JOHN O'CONNOR IN THE BAR of San Francisco's Olympic Club in the summer of 1967, and when he shook my hand, he almost crushed it. Big guy, size-18 neck, 46-inch chest, still an active AAU wrestler at 40. On the bridge of his nose was a telltale helmet scar. "Where'd you play football?" I asked. "Notre Dame, '46 and '47," he said. "Greatest collection of college football talent in history," I said. "How much did you play?"

"Not at all—for the varsity," he said. "B team. Scrimmaged against the big boys every day." He paused. "The greatness of those teams will never be realized. You ever hear of Art Statuto?"

Sure I had. He was the classic example of the postwar talent amassed by Irish coach Frank Leahy. Statuto never earned a monogram at Notre Dame, but he played three years of pro football afterward.

"We had lots of Art Statutos," O'Connor said.

The players fought for positions, playing time, a monogram, a smile from the coach. "There have been great college teams through the years," says Leon Hart, an All-America end at Notre Dame and the last lineman to win the Heisman Trophy, in 1949. "But for a sheer collection of talent, nothing could match our teams of '46 and '47."

Which team was better? Hard to say. Both were national champs, both were unbeaten, although the '46 team was held to a scoreless tie by the Doc Blanchard–Glenn Davis Army outfit. The statistics of the '46 Irish were eye-popping: No. 1 nationally in total offense and defense, first in rushing offense, fifth in rushing defense, third in pass defense, only 24 points (four touchdowns, no extra points) allowed during the nine-game season. The stats of the '47 squad were slightly less impressive, as the Irish finished second to the Michigan single-wing machine in total offense but ranked in the Top 10 in seven categories, including, for the first time, passing offense. Notre Dame gave up eight touchdowns and 52 points for the season. In each season the Irish never trailed in a game.

Most veterans of both teams give a slight nod to the '47 squad. "We were better, we'd played two years together," says Bill (Moose) Fischer, the All-America guard and winner of the '48 Outland Trophy as the nation's best lineman.

Leahy's biggest problem was sorting out all the talent that came back from the war, so in '46 he played his first unit, on both offense and defense, in the first and third quarters, the second group in the second and fourth. "It was a tremendous advantage to play on that second unit," says George Ratterman, who split quarterback duty with All-America Johnny Lujack in '46. "The first unit would beat hell out of them. We'd come in against guys who were worn out. Look it up. We scored twice as much as the firsts did."

"I was one of the few players who hadn't been in the service," says Hart, who arrived at Notre Dame as a 17-year-old freshman in '46 and would become one of the school's greatest stars ever. "I was one of 21 ends, 11 of them monogram winners." Nine players on the '47 Irish team were All-America at some point in their careers; two of them, Lujack and Hart, won the Heisman; two more, Fischer and George Connor, earned the Outland Trophy. Seven would be chosen for the College Football Hall of Fame. Who were the superstars? Hart, of course, a 6' 4", 252-pound end who made All-Pro with the Detroit Lions on offense and defense, just as Connor did for the Chicago Bears. And Lujack, the Bears' All-Pro quarterback who was equally gifted at defensive back.

Connor, a member of the NFL Hall of Fame, was the finest interior lineman in Notre Dame history, a demon blocker with enough speed to make All-Pro as a linebacker. The other big stars were Marty Wendell, a short, blocky guard and linebacker with a devastating initial pop, and Jim Martin, an end with an interior lineman's body.

"What I remember is that we fought every day—fought to win a job and then to hold it," says Martin, who went to Notre Dame after serving as a Marine in the Pacific, where he was decorated for swimming ashore and doing reconnaissance before the invasion of Tinian. "I was a mature 22-year-old freshman. You had guys like me, and then you had the older service vets, and practice was tough on them. They'd had enough of war, but that's what practice was every day, a war."

What the hell, the Notre Dame reserves were better than other people's first teams. Someone once asked right tackle Ziggy Czarobski what was the toughest team he had faced. "The Notre Dame second unit," he said. . . .

THE IRISH backfield included a mind-boggling array of talent, including Emil Sitko, who trampled Northwestern for 107 yards in a 27–0 whipping in '46.

2006 | A SLOPPY scrum engulfed Bates ballcarrier Jamie Walker as he churned out
one of his 43 carries during a four-overtime, 10-7 loss to Colby. | *Photograph by* DARYN SLOVER

1997 | THE STIFF ARM of Syracuse running back Kyle McIntosh administered a vigorous brush-off to Wisconsin's LaMar Campbell. | *Photograph by* DAMIAN STROHMEYER

1997 | THIS WRESTLING match was won by Michigan's pile-driving All-Big Ten tackle Jon Jansen when he pinned Colorado's Nick Ziegler. | *Photograph by* JOHN BIEVER

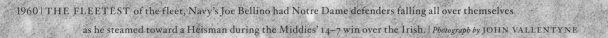

1960 | THE FLEETEST of the fleet, Navy's Joe Bellino had Notre Dame defenders falling all over themselves as he steamed toward a Heisman during the Middies' 14–7 win over the Irish. | *Photograph by* JOHN VALLENTYNE

> THE ALL-DECADE TEAM

	FIRST TEAM		SECOND TEAM
E	**Don Hutson** ALABAMA	E	**Larry Kelley** YALE
E	**Gaynell Tinsley** LSU	E	**Joe Skladany** PITTSBURGH
T	**Ed Widseth** MINNESOTA	T	**Nick Drahos** CORNELL
T	**Bruiser Kinard** MISSISSIPPI	T	**Joe Stydahar** WEST VIRGINIA
G	**Joe Routt** TEXAS A&M	G	**Bill Corbus** STANFORD
G	**Biggie Munn** MINNESOTA	G	**Bob Suffridge** TENNESSEE
C	**Alex Wojciechowicz** FORDHAM	C	**Ki Aldrich** TCU
B	**Sammy Baugh** TCU	B	**Davey O'Brien** TCU
B	**Nile Kinnick** IOWA	B	**Marshall Goldberg** PITTSBURGH
B	**Clint Frank** YALE	B	**John Kimbrough** TEXAS A&M
B	**Tom Harmon** MICHIGAN	B	**Byron White** COLORADO

> NICKNAMES <

Marshall [Biggie] Goldberg ∧
Charles [Ki] Aldrich
[Slingin'] Sammy Baugh
Madison [Moanin' Matty] Bell
George [Bad News] Cafego
Sam [The Tiburon Terror] Chapman
Clarke [The Lackawanna Express] Hinkle
Millard Fillmore [Dixie] Howell
[Jarrin'] John Kimbrough
Francis [Pug] Lund
Edgar [Eggs] Manske
Leo [Dutch] Meyer
James [Monk] Moscrip
Bob [The General] Neyland
Davey [Slingshot] O'Brien
Clarence [Ace] Parker
Harry [Blackjack] Smith
Clyde [Bulldog] Turner
Lynn [Pappy] Waldorf
Irvine [Cotton] Warburton
Byron [Whizzer] White

NATIONAL CHAMPION, COACH	HEISMAN WINNER

'30	**NOTRE DAME**	Knute Rockne
'31	**USC**	Howard Jones
'32	**USC, MICHIGAN**	Howard Jones, Harry Kipke
'33	**MICHIGAN**	Harry Kipke
'34	**MINNESOTA**	Bernie Bierman
'35	**MINNESOTA**	Bernie Bierman
'36	**MINNESOTA**	Bernie Bierman
'37	**PITTSBURGH**	Jock Sutherland
'38	**TCU**	Dutch Meyer
'39	**TEXAS A&M**	Homer Norton

First presented in 1935 by New York's Downtown Athletic Club to honor the nation's outstanding player, the DAC Trophy was renamed the Heisman Memorial Trophy in 1936 to honor longtime football innovator John W. Heisman, who died that year.

JAY BERWANGER	Chicago
LARRY KELLEY	Yale >
CLINT FRANK (14)	Yale >
DAVEY O'BRIEN	TCU
NILE KINNICK	Iowa

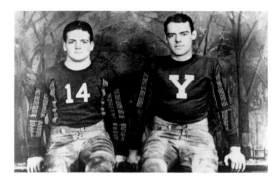

>> THE DECADE'S DYNASTIES

Minnesota

Bernie Bierman's Gophers were golden, winning national titles in 1934, '35 and '36. Their single-wing attack was run to perfection by tailback Pug Lund, and the defense held foes to less than 20 points in every game from '33 to the middle of '39.

USC

The "Thundering Herd" of Howard Jones went undefeated twice, won national titles in 1931 and '32 and was in the running again in '39. The '32 team, with glamour boy Cotton Warburton working behind the nation's strongest line, surrendered 13 points all season and thumped Pitt 35–0 in the Rose Bowl.

Tennessee

Bob Neyland's late-decade Volunteers won 23 straight games, going 11–0 in 1938 and whipping Oklahoma 17–0 in the Orange Bowl. The next season All-America guards Ed Molinski and Bob Suffridge, and back George Cafego led Tennessee to the last unscored-upon regular season in major college history.

Pittsburgh

Two-time All-America Marshall Goldberg was the main man in the Dream Backfield that ran Pitt to the national title in 1937. From 1930 to '38, Jock Sutherland's last year in charge, the Panthers were 70-10-7.

TCU >

There was no shortage of star power in Fort Worth, with QBs Sammy Baugh and Davey O'Brien, and center Ki Aldrich all suiting up for the Horned Frogs. Heisman winner O'Brien and Aldrich helped coach Dutch Meyer win the '38 national title.

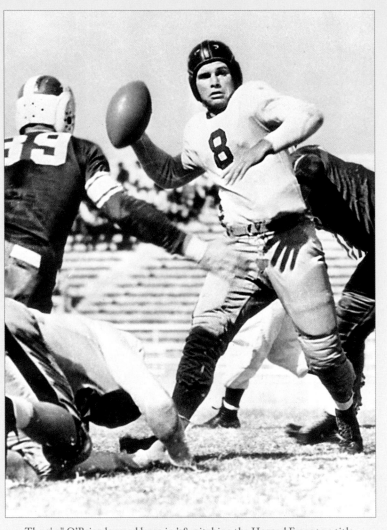

The 5' 7" O'Brien loomed large in '38, pitching the Horned Frogs to a title.

> EPIC GAMES

< Notre Dame *vs.* Ohio State

November 2, 1935

Trailing Tippy Dye *(with ball)* and Ohio State 13–0 at the half, the Irish rallied but still were staring at a 13–12 deficit when quarterback Andy Pilney went down with a knee injury with 50 seconds left in the game. His replacement, Bill Shakespeare, lofted a 19-yard pass over the Buckeyes' defense to pull out the heroic 18–13 win.

Pittsburgh *vs.* Fordham

October 16, 1937

Marshall Goldberg and his high-powered Panthers arrived in New York having outscored their first three foes 85–0 and having played scoreless ties the past two years against the Rams and their Seven Blocks of Granite. In the second quarter a Goldberg touchdown was called back for holding. The final: 0–0 again, the lone blemish on either team's '37 record.

Duke vs. USC

January 1, 1939 • ROSE BOWL

Neither the Trojans nor the unbeaten Blue Devils could muster any offense through three quarters. Duke, which hadn't allowed a point all season, took a 3–0 lead early in the fourth, but with 20 seconds separating the Blue Devils from perfection, USC scored on a 19-yard TD pass from fourth-string QB Doyle Nave to Al Krueger for the 7–3 win.

> CAMPUS CULTURE

YOU'VE GOT TO . . .

READ IT: *The Good Earth*, Pearl S. Buck; *Gone with the Wind*, Margaret Mitchell; *How To Win Friends and Influence People*, Dale Carnegie; *Brave New World*, Aldous Huxley

HEAR IT: Benny Goodman, Cole Porter, Duke Ellington, Bing Crosby, Glenn Miller, Ella Fitzgerald, Irving Berlin, George Gershwin, Johnny Mercer, Aaron Copland

SEE IT: *Dracula, King Kong, The Hunchback of Notre Dame, A Day at the Races, The Mummy, The Wizard of Oz, Mutiny on the Bounty, Mr. Smith Goes to Washington*

DISCUSS IT: The New Deal, Hitler, Admiral Byrd, Amelia Earhart, Jesse Owens in Berlin, N.Y. World's Fair, Empire State Building, end of Prohibition

"The only thing we have to fear is fear itself— nameless, unreasoning, unjustified terror which paralyzes needed efforts to convert retreat into advance."

—*Franklin D. Roosevelt in his first Inaugural Address, confronting the Great Depression, March 4, 1933*

DEAL WITH IT: The Depression, The Dust Bowl, the *Hindenburg*, isolationism

HAVE IT: Radio set, nylons, jackknife, Scotch tape, frozen food, *Superman* comic book

WEAR IT: Fedora, zippers, sweater vests, three-piece suits

DO IT: Cocktail parties, stamp collecting, playing the horses, Monopoly, miniature golf

Balancing the books was a faddishly extracurricular way to achieve model posture.

> SMARTEST GUY IN THE WORLD

ALBERT EINSTEIN The German-born physicist's theory of relativity unleashed atomic power. Though a lifelong pacifist, Einstein used his prestige to help persuade FDR to build an atomic bomb before the Nazis could.

> BY THE NUMBERS

13.4 Career yards per completion for Columbia quarterback Sid Luckman, third in the Heisman voting in 1938 despite playing for a 3–6 Lions team.

50 Years that Don Hutson's 165 receiving yards for Alabama against Stanford in 1935 would stand as a Rose Bowl record.

1 Inch of reduction in the circumference of a regulation football for the 1934 season, making passing easier.

69.9 Yards per game allowed by the 1937 Santa Clara defense, the alltime low. The 8–0 Broncos also led the nation in scoring defense (1.1 points per game) and rushing defense (25.3 yards average).

13 Schools that left the Southern Conference following the 1932 season to form the Southeastern Conference.

50 Range in miles of the first telecast of a college football game, between Fordham and Waynesburg on Sept. 30, 1939, at New York's Triborough Stadium.

INNOVATOR

Clark Shaughnessy While coaching at Chicago, Shaughnessy resuscitated and updated the old T formation, in which the quarterback (not the tailback) receives the center snap, paving the way for the modern passing game.

1989 | LAST STAND: Bo Schembechler, flanked by wideout Chris Calloway (2) and defensive tackle Brent White (88), led Michigan into battle against Ohio State at the Big House in his final regular-season game. | *Photograph by* SAM ABELL

1930s | THE STATE-OF-THE-ART pads worn by Duke's All-America tailback Ace Parker absorbed

hits on hips that swiveled to a 105-yard kickoff return for a TD against North Carolina in 1936. | *Photograph by* DAVID BERKWITZ

1978 | THE COOL of Joe Montana was already on display during a Notre Dame year that would peak with an epic Cotton Bowl comeback. | *Photograph by* MARVIN E. NEWMAN

1983 | THE HANDS of Jerry Rice made 102 catches for 1,450 yards on the season for Mississippi Valley State, both NCAA records. | *Photograph by* MARK PERLSTEIN

ROCK OF AGES

BY COLES PHINIZY

His oratory is legendary, but it was tactical genius that made Knute Rockne the greatest coach of all time.

–from SI, SEPTEMBER 10, 1979

ALTHOUGH DEVOID OF COLOR and sound, the old, grainy newsreel movies of Knute Rockne's men in action are still a thing of beauty. The line sets up; the backfield moves into the T formation. Then, with each man traveling a different distance with a different number of steps, as if guided by inner music, the backfield flows out of the T into the famous trapezoidal "Notre Dame box." In the next instant the ball is centered, and the backs are off, still in perfect unison, each on a different mission.

Since the early 1900s there had been many shift formations, simple and fancy, but none created as much of a stir as the Notre Dame shift installed by Rockne's predecessor Jesse Harper and exploited by Rockne. Working on the theory that the Notre Dame shift gave the Irish offense the advantage of having momentum when the ball was snapped, the rules makers of the 1920s twice tightened the restrictions on shifts. The original injunction that every man's feet be solidly planted before the snap was modified to prohibit even the slightest swaying of the body. Later, the rules were amended again, stipulating a full second without any motion. In spite of the restrictions, Notre Dame kept on winning.

Throughout the haggling, Rockne insisted that the virtue of the shift was not momentum but the advantage gained from perfect timing and execution. When Illinois coach Bob Zuppke protested that momentum was at issue, Rockne reputedly replied, "My good friend Zuppke knows that the only creature that can make forward progress by moving sideways is a crab." It was not a system worth much to mediocre teams with lone stars. It was designed for 11 men working as one. That was Rockne's credo, and it was far more a factor in Notre Dame's winning than his occasional harangues or psychological ploys.

Under Rockne, Notre Dame players came and went, but for nearly 20 years the off-tackle play "Old 51" lived on. It was the epitome of simple success based on timing and execution. When a key block was muffed, Old 51 often went nowhere. When everyone got his man—and most of the blocking was one-on-one—it was a long gainer. Rival teams came to know Old 51 and to recognize it by its call. They designed defenses specifically for it. Still it worked. Other coaches adopted Old 51, which provoked Rockne to grouse, "If they are going to use it, at least they could give it a different number."

When Notre Dame and Army met late in the 1926 season, both were undefeated. In the first half, Army contained Notre Dame by dropping its tackles off the line to defend against Old 51. In the second half, when Irish right end John Wallace reported that Army's left tackle, a Texan named Mortimer (Bud) Sprague, had moved back up on the line, the next play quarterback Red Edwards called was Old 51 to the right. That year Christy Flanagan, also a Texan, was the back who carried the ball on that play. Reviewing the game, sportswriter Tim Cohane reported, "That one play was enough. It was a perfect play. After a scoreless first half, Christy Flanagan, Notre Dame's left halfback, broke off Army's left tackle and ran 63 yards for a touchdown. The blocking, both in the line and downfield, eradicated every potential Cadet tackler, so that Christy went his way without so much as a finger being laid on him."

Final score: Notre Dame 7, Army 0.

When Notre Dame and Army met at Soldier Field in Chicago late in the 1930 season, again they were both undefeated. It was a wretched day; icy rain fell on a fog-shrouded field that was partly frozen and mostly mush. Army gained 63 yards on the ground, Notre Dame 188, most of it with Old 51.

With only five minutes to go, Old 51 was the difference. In his game story, Robert Kelley of *The New York Times* wrote, "For one play Marchmont Schwartz, Notre Dame's left halfback, found the stage completely arranged for him, and he ran 54 yards to a touchdown over turf that was as slippery as an ice rink . . . . Schwartz went off tackle. It was the perfect play toward which Notre Dame aims through all its games." Final score: Notre Dame 7, Army 6.

To succeed with a play as shopworn as Old 51, a coach needs 11 good men. "Football is not and should not be a game for the strong and stupid," Rockne observed. "It should be a game for the smart, the swift, the brave and the clever boy." . . .

RENOWNED FOR his inspirational words, Rockne (shown here at a '20s scrimmage) was also a sharp-eyed tactician, which helped him build a 105-12-5 record.

1998 | OHIO STATE'S Percy King took one for the team when he blocked the punt of Penn State's Pat Pidgeon in the Buckeyes' 28–9 win. | *Photograph by* AL TIELEMANS

1889 | SOMEHOW, ROCHESTER (white jerseys) stuck with football after losing its third game ever to Cornell by either 106 or 124 points—accounts vary. | *Photograph by* BROWN BROTHERS

1959 | A TIP by Oklahoma's Jerry Tillery (89) did not keep Texas's Bobby Lackey's extra point from getting over the crossbar in the Longhorns' 19–12 win. | *Photograph by* JOHN G. ZIMMERMAN

A LIFE CUT SHORT

BY WILLIAM NACK

Before his death from leukemia at age 23, Ernie Davis had become not only the first black player to win the Heisman Trophy but also the most beloved athlete in Syracuse history.

—*from* SI, SEPTEMBER 4, 1989

ERNIE DAVIS WAS AN IDEAL black football prospect at a time when racially skittish colleges were just beginning to integrate their teams. He was well suited to carry on at Syracuse, which Jim Brown had left three years before. But Brown ran into more than tackling dummies and opposing linemen in his years at Syracuse. Shortly before he arrived, another black Syracuse football player, Avatus Stone, had scandalized the school by indulging in what was perceived at the time to be an unseemly social life. "He dated a blonde majorette," says Brown. When Brown got to Syracuse, the caution light was on. He was watched as if he were an alien who had descended on the town in a pod from outer space. "They didn't want me at the start. But they finally accepted me," Brown says now. "And we had some success. I set records. We went to the Cotton Bowl, got on national television, and I didn't mess with the white girls on campus. Then they gave me the privilege of helping them recruit Ernie Davis. That meant they had finally accepted black players and wanted black players. Here they had a chance to get a player that fit all the molds and parameters they had." With Brown's help, Ben Schwartzwalder, the Syracuse coach, recruited Davis tirelessly. Says Brown, "They got him: Ernie Davis. And Ernie made it beautiful for that new era of championship guys. Dynamite dudes, black guys, came to Syracuse after Ernie. Floyd Little and Jim Nance and others. It was fantastic. They could go there without losing their dignity. I was fighting every day at Syracuse to hold on to my dignity. I broke through, but Ernie created the new era. Ernie was Ben's man. Schwartzwalder loved him."

Indeed, they all did, from the moment he hit the campus and first suited up for freshman football. In all his 25 years as a college coach, Schwartzwalder says, he never met another player like him. "Ernie was just like a puppy dog, friendly and warm and kind," he says. "He had that spontaneous goodness about him. He radiated enthusiasm. His enthusiasm rubbed off on the kids. Oh, he'd knock you down, but then he'd run back and pick you up. We never had a kid so thoughtful and polite. Ernie would pat the guys on the back who had tackled him and help them up. And compliment them: 'Great tackle.' Even opponents had a kindly feeling for him. They'd come into the dressing room after the game to see him. Jim Brown, Floyd Little and Larry Csonka would knock you down and run over you because they didn't like you. You were enemy. Ernie didn't dislike anybody. He'd knock you down and run over you because of his enthusiasm. If there was ever a perfect kid, it was Ernie Davis. He was the best kid I ever had anything to do with."

And he could play, to be sure, as grindingly hard as any of them. In his sophomore year, Davis carried 98 times for 686 yards—seven yards a carry—and scored 10 touchdowns as Syracuse went undefeated in the regular season, 10–0, and won its only national championship. Davis pulled a hamstring several days before Syracuse was to meet Texas in the Cotton Bowl in the final game of the season, and there was some doubt as to whether he could even play. But play he did. On Syracuse's first possession, running back Ger Schwedes threw an option pass to Davis, who was running a deep pattern, and the young halfback, limping noticeably, took off down the sideline. Fearing that Davis would reinjure the hamstring, Schwartzwalder ran after him, screaming, "Slow down, Ernie! Don't pull it!"

Davis limped into the end zone, completing a 57-yard run and an 87-yard play from scrimmage that was then the longest touchdown pass in the history of any major bowl. And despite his tender leg, he kept on playing, both ways. It was a vicious, meanly played game, with Texas players baiting the Orangemen with racial slurs, but Davis played as if unfazed by them. He scored one more touchdown, set up a third with an interception from his defensive back spot and scored twice on two-point conversions. Syracuse won 23–14.

Two years later, after junior and senior years as an All-America, Davis was awarded the Heisman, which confirmed that he was the finest running back in college football. Brown's Syracuse records were now his—2,386 rushing yards, a 6.6-yard average per carry, 35 touchdowns and 220 points. Of course he would be the most sought-after player in the NFL draft. Davis and his college roommate, tight end John Mackey, used to talk for hours about what life would be like in the National Football League. "We were just kids," says Mackey, "lying in bed, wondering if we'd be friends forever."

"Oh, yeah," Davis said. "We will be friends forever." . . .

A THREAT to score whenever he touched the ball, Davis linked a Syracuse dynasty that began with Brown and continued with Little and Csonka.

1956 | WOLVERINE WINGMEN Tom Maentz (85) and All-America Ron Kramer were the living ends in a 7–2 year for Michigan. | *Photograph by* JOHN G. ZIMMERMAN

1956 | TENNESSEE TITANS (from left) Johnny Majors, Buddy Cruze and John Gordy put their best faces forward before a 10–0 season. | *Photograph by* GABRIEL BENZUR

from MY, HOW HE DOES RUN ON
BY MYRON COPE | *SI, November 8, 1976*

TWO WEEKS AGO PITTSBURGH'S TONY Dorsett tore through and around Navy's defenses for the 180 yards that established him as the most prolific runner in the history of major college football. Down in the visitors' locker room after that game, Dorsett listened thoughtfully as Bill Hillgrove of Pittsburgh's WTAE concluded his radio interview. "In my estimation," Hillgrove declared, "you are the greatest back to ever play the game."

"Well," said Tony, "my stats prove it."

Lovers of humility may have bristled, but Tony was not yet through. Hustled before the press, he proclaimed that his career rushing yardage—then 5,206, or 29 yards more than Archie Griffin had accumulated at Ohio State en route to a couple of Heisman trophies—hardly quenched his thirst. He would feel fulfilled, he said, if he could push the record so high that he could safely assume nobody would break it until after the world had scattered dirt on his grave. About 6,000 yards would be nice, he suggested. That figure would require him to average a stunning 198.5 yards in his four remaining regular-season games. Still, he considered the goal realistic.

Alas, such declarations stamp Dorsett in the minds of many as a smart aleck while the fact is that ordinarily he is a young man of proper reserve, greatly beloved by his teammate who ranged the sideline as he bore in on Griffin's record at Annapolis, chorusing, "Go, Hawk, go!" What Pitt coach Johnny Majors turned loose three years ago is a muscular but lithe Panther—a dark, dimpled, handsome figure up from 157 pounds as a freshman to 185 pounds of speed and surprising inside power, who fits the words once spoken by Penn State's Joe Paterno as he gazed upon a tight end named Ted Kwalick. "What God had in mind there," said Paterno, "was a football player." If so, God was twice as earnest about the superbly equipped Dorsett. But why a goal of 6,000?

"It's just because I love the game," he answers, without affectation. "It's been a major part of my life, and every time I do something that a lot of people recognize, I'm going to take pride in it. And no matter how long or how much I've been into this game, I'll take pride in every record I set. I wanted to be known as Number 1, and I want to be known as that as long as I live." . . .

1976 | DORSETT WAS a Panther on the prowl during his Heisman-winning season, when he rushed for 1,948 yards, giving him a career-record total of 6,082. | *Photograph by* JAMES DRAKE

6 7 8 9

B

1972| EVEN AN umbrella defense would have proved unavailing when Fordham visited Baker Field and was swamped by Columbia 44–0. | *Photograph by* JAMES DRAKE

1956 | GAP-TOOTHED GUARD Chuck Maxime put some bite into the offensive line of Auburn's powerful Tigers. | *Photograph by* AUBURN UNIVERSITY

1965 | A TRUE spartan, Patrick Gallinagh helped plug the middle of the defensive line for Michigan State's national champions. | *Photograph by* WALTER IOOSS JR.

>THE ALL-DECADE TEAM

	FIRST TEAM		SECOND TEAM
E	**Leon Hart** NOTRE DAME	E	**Hub Bechtol** TEXAS
E	**Barney Poole** MISSISSIPPI, ARMY, UNC	E	**Bill Swiacki** COLUMBIA, HOLY CROSS
T	**Leo Nomellini** MINNESOTA	T	**Don Whitmire** NAVY, ALABAMA
T	**Dick Wildung** MINNESOTA	T	**George Connor** HOLY CROSS, NOTRE DAME
G	**Bill Fischer** NOTRE DAME	G	**Warren Amling** OHIO STATE
G	**Alex Agase** ILLINOIS, PURDUE	G	**Bill Fischer** NOTRE DAME
C	**Chuck Bednarik** PENN	C	**Clayton Tonnemaker** MINNESOTA
B	**Johnny Lujack** NOTRE DAME	B	**Angelo Bertelli** NOTRE DAME
B	**Doc Blanchard** ARMY	B	**Frankie Albert** STANFORD
B	**Glenn Davis** ARMY	B	**Charlie Trippi** GEORGIA
B	**Doak Walker** SMU	B	**Charlie Justice** NORTH CAROLINA

>NICKNAMES<

Elroy [Crazy Legs] Hirsch ∧
Vince [Bananas] Banonis
Chuck [Concrete Charlie] Bednarik
Angelo [The Springfield Rifle] Bertelli
Felix [Doc; Mr. Inside] Blanchard
[Pitchin'] Paul Christman
[Chuckin'] Charlie Conerly
Glenn [Mr. Outside] Davis
Chalmers [Bump] Elliott
[Automatic] Otto Graham
Tom [Old 98] Harmon
Charlie [Choo Choo] Justice
Leo [The Lion] Nomellini
Kyle [The Mighty Mustang] Rote
Clyde [Smackover] Scott
Frank [Fireball Frankie] Sinkwich
Emil [Six-Yard] Sitko
Norm [The Dutchman] Van Brocklin
[Squirmin'] Herman Wedemeyer
Albert [Ox] Wistert
Paul [Tank] Younger

	HEISMAN TROPHY WINNER	RUSHING LEADER	YARDS	PASSING LEADER	YARDS
'40	**TOM HARMON** Michigan	**AL GHESQUIERE** Detroit	957	**BILLY SEWELL** Washington State	1,023
'41	**BRUCE SMITH** Minnesota	**FRANK SINKWICH** Georgia	1,103	**BUD SCHWENK** Washington (St. Louis)	1,457
'42	**FRANK SINKWICH** Georgia	**RUDY MOBLEY** Hardin-Simmons	1,281	**RAY EVANS** Kansas	1,117
'43	**ANGELO BERTELLI** Notre Dame	**CREIGHTON MILLER** Notre Dame	911	**JOHNNY COOK** Georgia	1,007
'44	**LES HORVATH** Ohio State	**RED WILLIAMS** Minnesota	911	**PAUL RICKARDS** Pittsburgh	997
'45	**DOC BLANCHARD** Army	**BOB FENIMORE** Oklahoma A&M	1,048	**AL DEKDEBRUN** Cornell	1,227
'46	**GLENN DAVIS** Army	**RUDY MOBLEY** Hardin-Simmons	1,262	**TRAVIS TIDWELL** Auburn	943
'47	**JOHNNY LUJACK** Notre Dame	**WILTON DAVIS** Hardin-Simmons	1,173	**CHARLIE CONERLY** Mississippi	1,367
'48	**DOAK WALKER** SMU	**FRED WENDT** Texas Mines	1,570	**STAN HEATH** Nevada	2,005
'49	**LEON HART** Notre Dame	**JOHN DOTTLEY** Mississippi	1,312	**ADRIAN BURK** Baylor	1,428

>> THE DECADE'S DYNASTIES

Army >
Bolstered during wartime by recruits who could fulfill military commitments there, West Point thrived. The Cadets were unbeaten and won national titles in 1944 and '45. Backs Doc Blanchard (Mr. Inside) and Glenn Davis (Mr. Outside) earned Heisman Trophies in '45 and '46, respectively.

Notre Dame
With nine players finishing in the Top 10 in Heisman voting (including three winners: Angelo Bertelli '43, Johnny Lujack '47 and Leon Hart '49) and a record of 82-9-6, the Fighting Irish was one of the few teams to overcome wartime restrictions. Notre Dame went undefeated in five of the seven seasons that Frank Leahy was its coach.

Minnesota
In 1940 and '41 Bernie Bierman's undefeated Golden Gophers earned the school's fourth and fifth national titles in eight years, showcasing '41 Heisman back Bruce Smith.

Michigan
Finishing in the Top 10 every year, the Wolverines went 7–1 in 1940 with Heisman winner Tom Harmon. However, the highlight in Ann Arbor was a 25-game winning streak presided over by Fritz Crisler and Bennie Oosterbaan, each of whom produced a national championship ('47 and '48).

Iowa Pre-Flight
This was the best of the service-training teams that played primarily against depleted college squads. Under Bierman (in '42), Don Faurot ('43) and Jack Meagher ('44), the Seahawks went 26–5, outscored foes 801–315 and ranked No. 2 in '43.

Leading the Army juggernaut, Blanchard (35) and Davis each hauled in a Heisman.

> EPIC GAMES

<Army *vs.* Notre Dame
November 9, 1946

In their first game with full postwar squads, the nation's premier teams clashed at Yankee Stadium. The Cadets had won the previous two meetings by a combined score of 107–0 but were held to a scoreless tie as Doc Blanchard and Glenn Davis, were spiked by George Connor (81) and an Irish defense led by Johnny Lujack, also the Irish QB.

Stanford *vs.* Nebraska
January 1, 1941 • ROSE BOWL

Just 1-7-1 during the 1939 season, Stanford's "Wow Boys" in '40 rode coach Clark Shaughnessy's revolutionary T formation to a 9–0 record and a New Year's date with Nebraska. Trailing 13–7, the Indians overtook the Cornhuskers with a TD pass from QB Frankie Albert and a punt return for a score by Pete Kmetovic. The final: 21-13 Stanford.

Notre Dame vs. *SMU*
December 3, 1949

With Mustangs star Doak Walker sidelined, the Irish were a four-TD favorite in their season finale. But though flush with All-Americas and riding a 37-game undefeated streak, Notre Dame escaped Dallas with a 27–20 victory as an unheralded SMU sophomore, Kyle Rote, burst onto the scene by running for 115 yards and throwing for 146.

> CAMPUS CULTURE

YOU'VE GOT TO . . .

READ IT: *The Naked and the Dead*, Norman Mailer; *A Bell for Adano*, John Hersey; *Sexual Behavior in the Human Male*, Alfred Kinsey; *A Tree Grows in Brooklyn*, Betty Smith; *Native Son*, Richard Wright; *Nineteen Eighty-Four*, George Orwell

HEAR IT: Glenn Miller, Harry James, Frank Sinatra, Mel Torme, Duke Ellington, Nat King Cole, Ella Fitzgerald, Count Basie, The Andrews Sisters, Woody Guthrie, Tommy Dorsey, Jimmy Dorsey, The Ink Spots, Bing Crosby, Billie Holiday, Artie Shaw

SEE IT: *Citizen Kane, Casablanca, It's a Wonderful Life, The Philadelphia Story, The Maltese Falcon, The Pride of the Yankees, Double Indemnity, Notorious,* Hope and Crosby's *Road* movies, *Oklahoma, Miracle on 34th Street, White Heat*

"I have nothing to offer but blood, toil, tears and sweat."

—Winston Churchill in his first address to Parliament as British Prime Minister as the Nazis were rampaging through Western Europe, May 13, 1940

DISCUSS IT: The War effort, D-Day, G.I. Bill, Hiroshima and Nagasaki, Rosie the Riveter, Israel, the Marshall Plan, Berlin Blockade, The Iron Curtain, Jackie Robinson

DEAL WITH IT: Pearl Harbor, rationing, Nazi Germany, the Holocaust, FDR's death, Levittowns

HAVE IT: Pinups, electric razor, pea shooter, television, frozen dinners

WEAR IT: Zoot suit, fatigues, turtleneck sweaters, combat boots, bikinis

DO IT: Swallow goldfish, jitterbug, scrawl graffiti, eat at diners

PLAY IT: Slinky, radio, pinball, bridge

> SMARTEST GUY IN THE WORLD

J. ROBERT OPPENHEIMER An eminent researcher in astrophysics, nuclear physics, spectroscopy and quantum-field theory, Oppenheimer directed the supersecret Manhattan Project, whose success in developing the atomic bomb arguably hastened the end of World War II.

Not for the weak of stomach, goldfish-swallowing was one way in which coeds could belly-up with the big boys.

> BY THE NUMBERS

31 Head coaches who either played or began their coaching careers at Miami (Ohio), a.k.a. the Cradle of Coaches. Among them: Red Blaik, Paul Brown, Sid Gillman, Weeb Ewbank, Woody Hayes, Ara Parseghian, Bo Schembechler, Jim Tressel.

21.0 Yards per punt return for UCLA's Jackie Robinson in 1940, best in the nation.

40 Points for which Bobby Layne was responsible in Texas' 40-27 win over Missouri in the 1946 Cotton Bowl. Layne passed for two TDs, ran for three, caught one and booted four extra points.

117 Points scored by Michigan's Tom Harmon in 1940, making him the first to win back-to-back scoring titles. Oklahoma's Billy Sims would do it in '78 and '79.

575 Points by the College of the Pacific in 1949, an NCAA record. QB Eddie LeBaron led the 11–0 Tigers to 502.9 yards per game.

17 Service teams that played at least one season from 1942 through '45.

INNOVATOR
Red Blaik
The Army coach executed the first platoon system, inserting his best backs, Gil Stephenson and Jim Cain, only when the Cadets had the ball. Scorned by the two-way faithful, Blaik's scheme won games and acceptance.

1965 | TENNESSEE WINGBACK Hal Wantland took flight, but was dragged back to earth short of the goal line by Alabama's All-America linebacker Paul Crane in the Vols' 7–7 tie with the eventual national champion Crimson Tide. | *Photograph by* JAY LEVITON

2004 | THOROUGHLY MODERN, the bulletlike model looked positively retro on the bluefangled turf of Boise State's Bronco Stadium. | *Photograph by* JOHN BIEVER

> **Artifacts**

Pigskin Parade

With their evolving silhouettes and textures, these balls of fame help trace the story of the game

1906 | The squishy ball was not ideal for tossing, but the Elis won with the newly legal forward pass.

1919 | A Demon Deacon really put a devil of a boot to a spongy ball favoring the kicking game.

1924 | The names of the most storied backfield in history are arrayed in a box formation.

1934 | Lions halfback Al Barabas scored the only TD on a trick play in this epic upset.

1955 | You wouldn't know it by this score, but the streamlined shape made passing potent.

1969 | The eyes of Texas feasted upon a ball marking the Longhorns' second national title.

0:00 TO GO

BY GARY CARTWRIGHT

*During the 1990s time ran out on the Southwest Conference—
but what a time it was.* —*from* SI, OCTOBER 30, 1995

LET'S BURY THE OLD DEAR without getting maudlin. Date the obituary for the end of the 1995 college football season, football being the Southwest Conference's raison d'être and the only thing anyone will remember about it—except that at least one of its member schools was usually on probation and the majority of its players free on bond. Those of us who grew up with the Southwest Conference shed no tears for what it became but remember fondly what it was. From the time it was founded in 1915 until it began to fall apart in the '70s, the conference shaped our world and gave us stature. Until the second half of this century, Texas was a largely rural, largely homogeneous society. Despite our image of boisterous self-confidence, we Texans weren't sure if outsiders viewed us as rugged individualists or just hayseeds. For all of our rustic shortcomings, however, nobody played better football. Texas had the finest high school players in the country, and until the 1970s most of them stayed to play in the Southwest Conference. In the '30s SMU, TCU and Texas A&M each won a national title, and from '63 to '70, Darrell Royal's Texas teams won three. Those were the two golden eras of SWC football, but there were two others nearly as good: the postwar '40s, when SMU and Doak Walker battled Texas and Bobby Layne for state and national supremacy, and the mid- and late '50s, highlighted by Abe Martin's TCU teams.

As early as 1934 the air was literally filled with Southwest Conference football, thanks to the Humble Radio Network. You couldn't visit a drugstore or barbershop without hearing the roar of the crowd and the boom of the marching bands at Kyle Field or the Cotton Bowl—or the voice of Humble's master of word pictures, Kern Tips, saying, "They give the ball again to little Jimmy Swink, and this time he rides the back of big Norman Hamilton down to the four-, make that the three-yard line, where it's first-and-*goal* for the Froggies!"

You didn't have to be college-educated to have a favorite team. Bank presidents with degrees from SMU and pipe fitters who hadn't finished third grade displayed their choice in the form of pennant-shaped decals on the rear windows of their cars. Millions of Texans from Beaumont to Laredo to Amarillo never saw a game but lived and died from Saturday to Saturday with the Frogs, the Mustangs, the Bears, the Longhorns, the Aggies, the Owls, the Hogs—and later the Red Raiders and the Cougars.

The flavor of the conference came not so much from the coaches and the teams as from the customs and folk wisdom imparted by different groups of fans. It was said that TCU fans wore jeans and white socks and called each other Bubba and Betty Bob. SMU fans drank Chardonnay and lived off their trust funds. Baylor fans did not make love standing up, lest God mistake the act for dancing. Longhorns fans sipped tea and were insufferably high-handed. Aggies were zealots, superpatriots and bumpkins.

Even the cheerleaders matched their institutions. Texas's best-known cheerleaders from the 1950s and '60s were Kay Bailey Hutchison, Texas's first female senator, and Harley Clark, inventor of the "Hook 'em, Horns" sign and later a judge. SMU's best-known cheerleader was Aaron Spelling, now the titan of trash TV.

I'm not old enough to remember the 1930s, but I grew up on the legends. Sammy Baugh and John Kimbrough were more meaningful to me than Davy Crockett and Jim Bowie. Coaches Dutch Meyer of TCU and Matty Bell of SMU were good friends who fished together in the spring and tried to beat each other's ears off in the fall. Their '35 game was for the national championship, which SMU won.

The conference's second national champion was Meyer's 1938 TCU team, with the great Davey O'Brien at quarterback, but my favorite stories involved the Southwest Conference's third champions of that decade, the '39 Aggies. I heard about them from my old granny, who had become addicted to Texas A&M football as a girl when she watched the Fightin' Texas Aggie Band parade down Fort Worth's Main Street before a game at TCU. Though she never saw a game, Granny could recite plays from every Aggie season. "When time was a-runnin' out," she would tell me as I lay curled at her feet, "we give the ball to Jarrin' John Kimbrough, and he went and followed Marshall Robnett's block, bodies going this-a-way and that-a-way, plumb to the end zone." In the '40s and '50s, Granny and I listened to Aggie games on radio. Before each game she would kill a chicken and study the entrails, then place an appropriately colored candle in the window. When the Aggies scored, we would march around the room, waving maroon-and-white pennants and singing the *Aggie War Hymn* . . . .

AGGIE ALL-AMERICA Kimbrough carried A&M to a 13–12 victory over Fordham in the '41 Cotton Bowl while also toting the hopes of a hardscrabble region.

1983 | BO JACKSON outsprinted Auburn's foes on his way to a 6.6-yard career average and a narrow victory in the '85 Heisman vote. | *Photograph by* TONY TOMSIC

1956 | GOLDEN BOY Paul Hornung used Notre Dame spring drills as a springboard to the only Heisman won by a player from a losing team. | *Photograph by* JOHN G. ZIMMERMAN

1978 | THE 'DO of Oklahoma's Heisman winner Billy Sims, like the sight of him in the open field, was hair-raisin'. | *Photograph by* MALCOLM EMMONS

1988 | PITY THE poor fool who put a clip on Georgia linebacker Norman Cowins, he of the Mr. T-type mohawk. | *Photograph by* ANTHONY NESTE

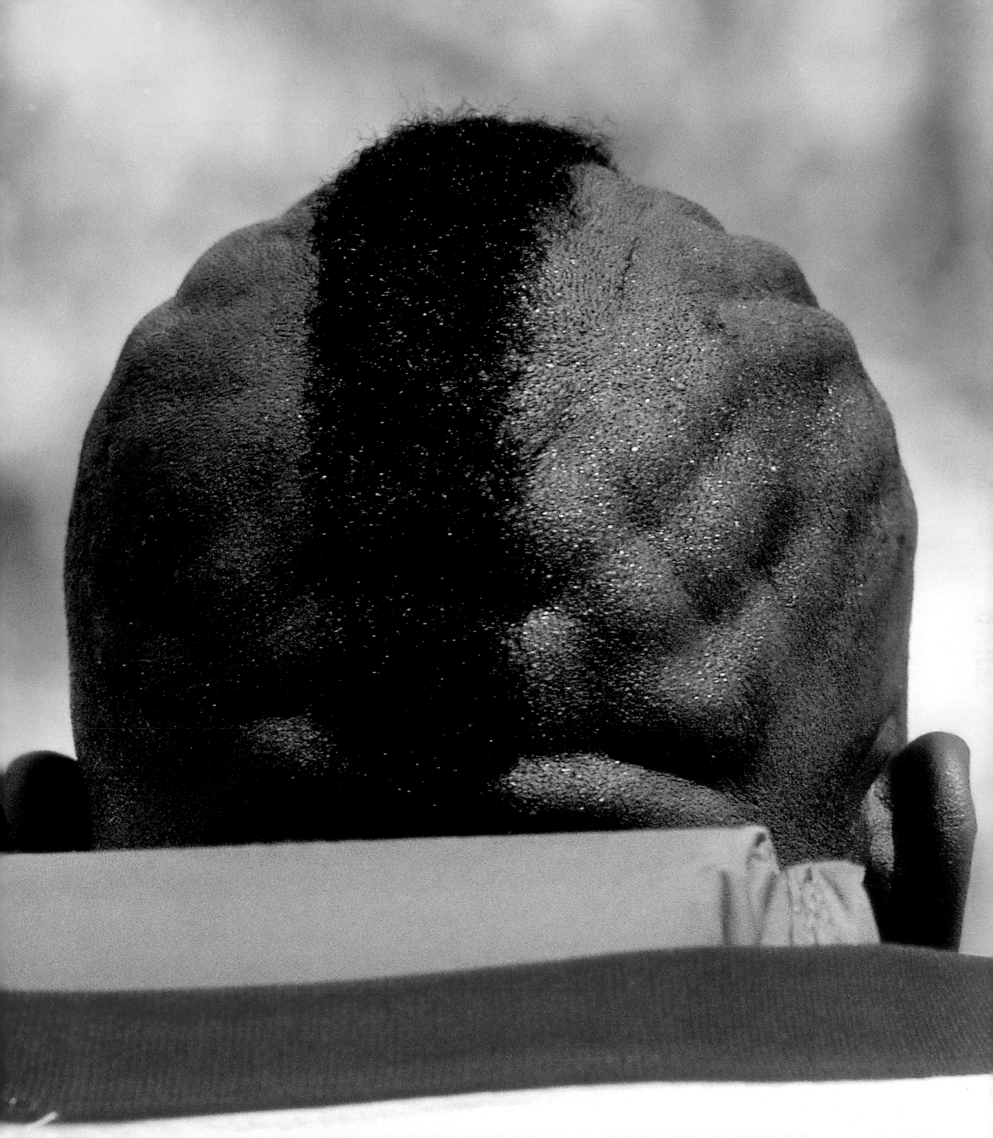

IT'S NOT JUST
A RUN OF LUCK

BY JOHN UNDERWOOD

There has to be an explanation for USC's illustrious dynasty at tailback, from Mike Garrett and O. J. Simpson to Ricky Bell and Charles White. —from SI, NOVEMBER 20, 1978

SINCE THE EARLY 1960S, THE University of Southern California has been winning football games and influencing poll takers with a modern folk hero known as the USC Tailback. According to his legend, the USC Tailback is a colossus who carries the ball 40 times a game and cannot be stopped with conventional weapons. Alexander the Great did not scorch as much earth as the USC Tailback. The USC Tailback rushes for around 1,000 yards a year and goes on to make all the All-teams and, eventually, a million dollars in the pros. His aliases are Mike Garrett, O. J. Simpson, Clarence Davis, Anthony Davis, Ricky Bell and Charles White. Two of the above (Garrett and Simpson) won Heisman Trophies. Two others (Anthony Davis and Bell) were runners-up. White is certain to come close, if not this year, then surely next, when he will be a senior. The USC Tailback has come to be what the Notre Dame quarterback (Bertelli, Lujack, Hornung, et al.) used to be: the glamour player–position of football.

USC Tailbacks have certain common denominators. They are all black. They are all tough. The first time a USC coach saw Clarence Davis play, Davis's front teeth were knocked out early in the game; he had his gums sewed up at halftime, and was back on the field for the second half. Ricky Bell, taken from a game when his shoulder popped out of its socket, jammed it back in place and complained to coach John Robinson, "Why did you take me out?"

They all come from urban Los Angeles, except Simpson, who grew up in urban San Francisco. All six were raised in low-income neighborhoods, in what sociologists call a "matriarchal environment" (i.e., their fathers weren't around much). But none of them remembers ever missing a meal, and all recall a fairly stable home life, with responsibilities. Responsibility, another common thread. But in the end the only similarity that counts is that all six of these remarkable men can run like hell.

If anything, the dissimilarities among the USC Tailbacks are more revealing. Or, at least, more interesting. To begin with, the six vary greatly in size and style. Garrett and Anthony Davis were tiny as tailbacks go (in the 5' 9", 180-pound class); Simpson, the "ideal," was 6' 2", 207 as an undergraduate; the menacing Ricky Bell, 6' 2", 220. Like Clarence Davis, White is of medium build (5' 11", 185), not split as high as Anthony Davis, but with a running style he copied watching AD in high school. Under way, the strides of these two become so elongated they appear to prance like drum majors.

Garrett, on the other hand, was a land crab who could scuttle almost as fast as he could run. Simpson, who was a world-class sprinter, was a sliding, gliding type who emerged from holes almost upright. If Simpson's battle hymn was a medley of pace and acceleration, Ricky Bell's was an anvil chorus. "Bell makes 'em pay for every inch," a USC coach used to say.

As for their statistics, they are not all that compelling. On the NCAA's alltime list of rushing leaders through 1977, which does not include bowl-game yardage, Tony Dorsett's record 6,082 yards is far ahead of Bell's 3,553 (15th), Anthony Davis' 3,426 (18th), Garrett's 3,221 (32nd) and Simpson's 3,124 (40th). Ed Marinaro's 209-yards-per-game single-season average is almost 40 yards better than Simpson's 170.9 and Bell's 170.5 (fourth and fifth on the list, respectively). It is the dependable, recurring presence of the USC Tailback in the record books that makes the position so special. That the individual also "rises to the position," as Robinson says, to become beloved as a leader and team man, or finds, as Bell did, "a source of strength" in it, is significant but beside the point. The point is that it is not their size, their temperament, their ability or even the speed with which they hurdle airport railings to get to the car-rental counter that sets them apart.

What distinguishes them is a very special set of circumstances that comes along every so often and makes football such a compelling game for those brooding masochists who sometimes coach it. Something happened to give life to the USC Tailback. It was a combination of the right coach (John McKay), the right philosophy (McKay's), the right formation (the power I, a McKay original) and, as the pièces de résistance, the right athletes. . . .

AMONG THE more diminutive of the storied Trojan tailbacks, the gamboling Anthony Davis otherwise fit the mold for USC's iconic offensive weapon.

2007 | MARCUS BARNETT of Cincinnati dreaded losing his hat when South Florida's Mike Jenkins hit him. | *Photograph by* CHRIS LIVINGSTON

2003 | COURTNEY TAYLOR of Auburn was riding without a helmet while he bulldogged USC's Jason Leach. | *Photograph by* DAVID E. KLUTHO

1995 | A FLING against Florida, his nemesis, was ultimately futile for Tennessee's Peyton Manning in a 62–37 loss at Gainesville. | *Photograph by* AL TIELEMANS

1988 | HITTING THE skids against Southern Cal, UCLA's Troy Aikman got the ball away before settling on the Rose Bowl turf. | *Photograph by* RICHARD MACKSON

HE'S TRACKING THE BEAR

BY RICK TELANDER

Having molded remarkable teams and young men at Grambling since 1941, Eddie Robinson was closing in on Bear Bryant's record for career victories. —*from* SI, SEPTEMBER 1, 1983

THE TOP OF THE LIST LOOKS like this: Bear Bryant (323), Amos Alonzo Stagg (314), Pop Warner (313), Eddie Robinson (305). Those are the career victory totals of the winningest college football coaches. No one else is even close to the top four. No. 5 is Woody Hayes, with 238. Three things about that list: First, the top three coaches are legends; second, they're white; third, they're deceased. Eddie Robinson, 64, athletic director and coach at Grambling State in Grambling, La., is black, largely unheralded and going strong. When he wins 19 more games to become the winningest college coach ever, he'll set a record that probably will never be matched. And some people aren't going to like it.

Says Penn State's Joe Paterno, 56, whose 162 victories make him the sixth-winningest active coach, "There will always be people who say Eddie's record isn't the real thing. But a win's a win. I don't care what league you're in. Anybody who resents his moment of glory would be an awfully small person."

What's remarkable about Eddie Robinson is that he has bridged so many eras so easily. When he started at Grambling, in 1941, he *was* the athletic department. He had just graduated from Leland College (now defunct) in Baker, La., where he'd been a tailback, fullback and punter, and was working at a feed mill when he heard about the Grambling opening. He applied and got the job largely because of his enthusiasm. Besides coaching football, Robinson had to coach baseball and men's and women's basketball and run the physical education department—all for $64 a month. "The word coach covered a lot more in those days," he says.

His recruits, mainly raw kids without a lot of choices, came from the farms and small towns of Louisiana. In the '40s many black high schools in the state began using Grambling's offensive sets, and the college's name was familiar to young athletes. Robinson sold their mothers and fathers on the integrity of his program and then stepped into the cotton fields to remind the youngsters where their loyalties lay.

One of his early players was a football and basketball star named Fred Hobdy, who has been the Grambling basketball coach since taking over for Robinson in 1956. "The thing about Eddie is that he's very modern," says Hobdy, who also serves as an assistant football coach. "He's the first one to say, 'We've got to change.' Take drinking water. Remember when you never had it on the field? He was one of the first coaches to bring it out. I said, 'No!' But he said, 'It'll make them play better.' And, of course, it did."

Another of Robinson's early players was Grambling president Joseph B. Johnson, who captained the basketball team in 1956–57. "What Eddie does is enable athletes to develop a pattern for living and thinking," says Johnson. "He tells you, 'You can do anything you want to if you work hard enough.' When I was playing, he wouldn't let you miss class. He's still that way. A kid can go anywhere he wants now, but what would we have become without Grambling and Eddie Robinson? We wouldn't have had a chance."

Rival coaches respect Robinson on a different level. "I'd always been told Grambling just had a lot of material, but I found out that's nonsense," says Jackson State coach W.C. Gorden, who has beaten Grambling just once in six attempts. "Defensively, when you play them you have to prepare a total, flexible game plan, because Eddie seems to have a play to counter any coverage or stunt. He's about the best I've seen at making adjustments during games."

Without question, Grambling doesn't get as many bluechippers as it once did. "The starting running backs at LSU might have come here in the past," says Robinson. Indeed, the defensive unit of Grambling's 1960 team featured four future All-Pros: Ernie Ladd, Buck Buchanan, Roosevelt Taylor and Willie Brown. It's generally accepted that on a given day several of Robinson's teams in the '60s could have beaten any school in the country. While that's no longer the case, he's more successful than ever now. From '53 to '72, the Tigers won 73% of their games. From '73 to '82 they won almost 80%. Robinson says he still gets some exceptional players because he's "lucky." Fact is, he still gets them because he's Eddie Robinson . . . .

A FORWARD thinker, Robinson (here in 1989) spent 55 seasons on the Grambling sideline, became the first to reach 400 wins—and put his school on the map.

1983 | CHAMPAIGN WAS bubbling over when Ilinois receiver David Williams tumbled into the end zone in a 16–6 win over Michigan. | *Photograph by* CARL SKALAK

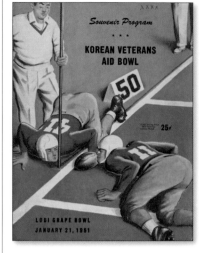

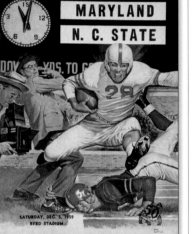

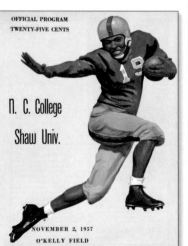

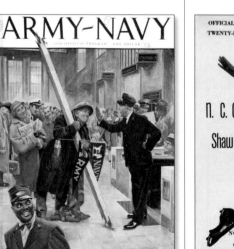

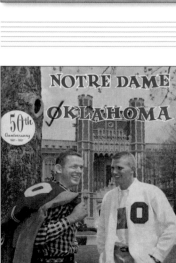

>THE ALL-DECADE TEAM

FIRST TEAM			SECOND TEAM	
E	Ron Beagle NAVY		E	Bill McColl STANFORD
E	Ron Kramer MICHIGAN		E	Dan Foldberg ARMY
T	Lou Michaels KENTUCKY		T	Jim Weatherall OKLAHOMA
T	Alex Karras IOWA		T	Dick Modzelewski MARYLAND
G	Les Richter CAL		G	Bud McFadin TEXAS
G	Jim Parker OHIO STATE		G	Calvin Jones IOWA
C	Jerry Tubbs OKLAHOMA		C	Maxie Baughan GEORGIA TECH
B	Jim Brown SYRACUSE		B	John David Crow TEXAS A&M
B	Billy Cannon LSU		B	Johnny Lattner NOTRE DAME
B	Howard Cassady OHIO STATE		B	Alan Ameche WISCONSIN
B	Babe Parilli KENTUCKY		B	Dick Kazmaier PRINCETON

>NICKNAMES<

Howard [Hopalong] Cassady ^
Harry [The Golden Greek] Agganis
Alan [The Horse] Ameche
[Jaguar] Jon Arnett
Don [Bull] Bosseler
Tom [Rock of Gibraltar] Brown
Charlie [Flavy] Flowers
Willie [Gallopin' Gal] Galimore
Wayne [The Thumper] Harris
Garney [Zoomer] Henley
Paul [The Golden Boy] Hornung
Alex [Mad Duck] Karras
Leo [The Minnesota Express] Lewis
Tommy [Shoo-Fly] McDonald
Hugh [The King] McElhenny
Jack [Gabby] Pardee
Vito [Babe] Parilli
Jim [The Rusk Rambler] Swink
Thad [Pie] Vann
Billy [Curly] Vessels
Charles [Bud] Wilkinson

	HEISMAN TROPHY WINNER		RUSHING LEADER	YARDS		PASSING LEADER	YARDS
'50	VIC JANOWICZ Ohio State		WILFORD WHITE Arizona State	1,502		DON HEINRICH Washington	1,846
'51	DICK KAZMAIER Princeton		OLLIE MATSON San Francisco	1,566		DON KLOSTERMAN Loyola Marymount	1,843
'52	BILLY VESSELS Oklahoma		HOWIE WAUGH Tulsa	1,372		DON HEINRICH Washington	1,647
'53	JOHNNY LATTNER Notre Dame		J.C. CAROLINE Illinois	1,256		BOB GARRETT Stanford	1,637
'54	ALAN AMECHE Wisconsin		ART LUPPINO Arizona	1,359		PAUL LARSON California	1,537
'55	HOWARD CASSADY Ohio State		ART LUPPINO Arizona	1,313		GEORGE WELSH Navy	1,319
'56	PAUL HORNUNG Notre Dame		JIM CRAWFORD Wyoming	1,104		JOHN BRODIE Stanford	1,633
'57	JOHN DAVID CROW Texas A&M		LEON BURTON Arizona State	1,126		KEN FORD Hardin-Simmons	1,254
'58	PETE DAWKINS Army		DICK BASS Pacific	1,361		BUDDY HUMPHREY Baylor	1,316
'59	BILLY CANNON LSU		PERVIS ATKINS New Mexico State	971		DICK NORMAN Stanford	1,963

>> THE DECADE'S DYNASTIES

Oklahoma >
You know that a program is special when a single defeat makes headlines. The Sooners of Bud Wilkinson (*right*) didn't drop a game from Oct. 3, 1953 to Nov. 16, 1957, a 48-game streak bookended by losses to Notre Dame. Toss in three national ('50, '55 and '56) and 10 conference titles, and Billy Vessels ('52 Heisman), Tommy McDonald, Jerry Tubbs and their mates might qualify as the most imposing dynasty of any decade.

Ohio State
In 1951 Woody Hayes took charge in Columbus—and how. With a smash-mouth style and stars like '55 Heisman winner Howard (Hopalong) Cassady, Hayes transformed the Buckeyes into the scourge of the Big Ten and a perennial national championship contender, ranking No. 1 in 1954 and '57.

Michigan State
Biggie Munn closed his career in 1953 having gone 35–2 in his last four seasons, winning the '52 national title with back Don McAuliffe as a spearhead. In '55 Duffy Daugherty's Spartans went 9–1 and beat UCLA in the Rose Bowl.

LSU
The Bayou Bengals clawed to the top using the heady coaching of Paul Dietzel, who masterminded an 11–0 season and a national title in '58 and the skills of back Billy Cannon, who in '59 swept all five regions in the Heisman voting.

Tennessee
In Bob Neyland's last three seasons (1950–52) the Vols won 29 of 34 games and a national title in '51. That success coincided with the career of the peerless tackle Doug Atkins.

With their epic streak, Wilkinson and his Sooners stood astride the game.

> EPIC GAMES

< Navy *vs.* Army
December 2, 1950

In arguably the rivalry's biggest upset—and with President Truman (*left,* with captains Dan Foldberg and Tom Bakke*)* looking on—the 2–6 Middies snapped the Cadets' 28-game winning streak with a 14–2 victory. Navy defenders, though allowing the vaunted Army offense inside the 20-yard line seven times in the second half, did not yield a score.

Oklahoma *vs.* Maryland
January 2, 1956 • ORANGE BOWL

In a head-on collision of winning streaks (Oklahoma's was at 29 games, Maryland's at 15), the Sooners steamrolled the Terps with superior speed and cinched the national title with a 20–6 victory. Little back Tommy McDonald was Oklahoma's big weapon, passing, returning punts and rushing for the TD that gave the Sooners the lead in the third quarter.

Notre Dame *vs.* Oklahoma
November 16, 1957

The Fighting Irish's Dick Lynch capped a 20-play, 80-yard fourth-quarter drive with a three-yard TD run around right end to give visiting Notre Dame a 7–0 win over the Sooners—the first defeat for Oklahoma since 1953, a record span of 47 games. The last team to have beaten Oklahoma? Notre Dame, 28–21, in the '53 opener, also at Norman.

> CAMPUS CULTURE

YOU'VE GOT TO . . .

READ IT: The *Catcher in the Rye*, J.D. Salinger; *The Man in the Gray Flannel Suit*, Sloan Wilson; *On the Road*, Jack Kerouac; *Lord of the Flies*, William Golding; *Atlas Shrugged*, Ayn Rand; *Naked Lunch*, William S. Burroughs; *The Power of Positive Thinking*, Norman Vincent Peale; *Lolita*, Vladimir Nabokov

HEAR IT: Elvis Presley, Chuck Berry, Buddy Holly, Jerry Lee Lewis, Miles Davis, Dave Brubeck, Fats Domino, Bo Diddley, Richie Valens, Nat King Cole, John Coltrane, Frank Sinatra

SEE IT: *Ben-Hur*, *The Bridge over the River Kwai*, *Singin' in the Rain*, *Some Like It Hot*, *From Here to Eternity*, *Rebel Without a Cause*, *The Ten Commandments*, *I Love Lucy*, *The Honeymooners*,

American Bandstand, *The Adventures of Ozzie and Harriet*, *The Ed Sullivan Show*, *The $64,000 Question*, *Superman*, *Candid Camera*

DISCUSS IT: Sputnik, Kinsey, beatniks, quiz-show scandals, Cold War, pop art, four-minute mile, Rosa Parks

"Whether you like it or not, history is on our side. We will bury you."
—Soviet Premier Nikita Khrushchev to Western diplomats at the Polish embassy in Moscow, Nov. 18, 1956

DEAL WITH IT: Korean War, baby boom, air-raid drills, Army-McCarthy hearings, "separate but equal," suburbia and conformity

HAVE IT: *Playboy*, transistor radio, polio vaccine, motorcycle

WEAR IT: Letterman's sweater, coonskin caps, saddle shoes, poodle skirts, thin neckties, leather jackets, crew cuts, white T-shirts, pegged blue jeans, Chuck Taylor All-Stars

DO IT: Panty raids, roller skating, sock hops, drive-ins, phone-booth cramming

PLAY IT: Hula-Hoop, boomerang, jukebox

"Cramming" took many forms: for exams, and into VWs and phone booths.

> SMARTEST GUY IN THE WORLD

JONAS SALK Tens of thousands died or were paralyzed each year from polio until this University of Pittsburgh–based physician developed the vaccine that helped eradicate the disease. When asked if he had patented his vaccine, Salk answered, "Could you patent the sun?"

> BY THE NUMBERS

60 Victories at Kentucky for Paul (Bear) Bryant—the winningest coach in Wildcats history—in eight seasons before he left in 1953.

93 Percent increase in made field goals in Division I games after the goal posts were widened in 1959 from 18' 6" to 23' 4".

1 Total weeks (Oct. 7–13, 1952) that Wisconsin has been ranked No. 1 in the history of the AP poll.

29 Career interceptions for Illinois defensive back Al Brosky from 1950 to '52, an NCAA record.

167 Yards by which San Francisco's Ollie Matson won the 1951 rushing title over Frank Goode of Hardin-Simmons. Matson ran for 174.0 yards per game, Goode for 116.6.

2 Consecutive Maxwell Awards won by Notre Dame halfback Johnny Lattner, in 1952 and '53—the only player to be honored twice.

8 Losses for Notre Dame in 1956 and '60, the worst seasons in Fighting Irish history.

INNOVATOR
Bud Wilkinson
By dropping the two ends off of a standard seven-man line, the Oklahoma coach unleashed his ferocious 5-2 defense, designed to funnel opposing runners to the middle by making it impossible to successfully attack the flanks.

from WOOFERS & TWEETERS

BY FRANZ LIDZ | *SI, October* 28, 1991

LIVE ANIMAL MASCOTS HAVE LONG been a part of college football, and they have come in amazing variety—from Arkansas razorbacks to Michigan wolverines, from Washington huskies to SMU mustangs. Predators are preferred—even nasty, disagreeable insects: yellow jackets (Georgia Tech), spiders (Richmond), hornets (Delaware State) and wasps (Emory and Henry College in Emory, Va.). Bug haters have a mascot of their own: the anteater (UC Irvine), which provokes the lusty cheer, "Give 'em the tongue! Zot! Zot!" Other foods are represented as well. To protest greater spending for athletics than for academics in 1971, Scottsdale (Ariz.) Community College students rallied behind an artichoke.

The artichoke's poise and physical toughness make it an ideal mascot. But the artichoke can't do half the tricks the U.S. Air Force Academy's falcons can. "We've got the only performing mascot act," says Tom Hermel, one of 11 cadets charged with caring for the birds. At halftime, two falcons wheel over the stadium, wings spread wide, as sleek and elegant and streamlined as F-14s approaching the deck of an aircraft carrier. They swoop down and try to strike a lure being twirled by a handler on the field. The lure is pulled away at the last second, and the falcons zoom back into the sky. "When we play Army, our cadets chant, 'Let's see the mule fly! Let's see the mule fly!' " says Hermel. And what do Army's cadets chant back? "Nothing special," says Hermel. "Usually just, 'Air Force sucks!' "

If a team doesn't play well, mascots are sometimes held accountable. The Livestock Club at Colorado State once proposed to butcher Cam the Ram V and raffle off his head. Cam V, it seems, had presided over six straight losing seasons. He died in 1973 at age seven of natural causes. In this era of sensitivity to animal rights, fewer and fewer beasties sniff and soar and slither around the sidelines. Those that remain inspire fierce loyalty. Hundreds of humans gathered last year in Athens, Ga., as Uga (pronounced *ugga*) IV, the Georgia bulldog, was laid to rest in Sanford Stadium in a red-and-black plywood coffin.

Uga IV's passing was a shame, but how do you explain the 20,000 mourners who turned out in 1989 to see Texas A&M's collie, Reveille IV, buried with full military honors? The world has surely gone to the dogs . . . and the goats . . . and the artichokes. . . .

2003 | AT COLORADO'S Folsom Field, generations of Ralphies (here, III) and their predecessors have led the Buffs' charge onto the field before each half since 1934. | *Photograph by* MICHAEL MARTIN

1957 | IN A tense and timeless tableau, homespun coach Abe Martin gave pregame instructions to his TCU team before the Horned Frogs went out and defeated Jim Brown and Syracuse 28–27 in the Cotton Bowl. | *Photograph by* MARVIN E. NEWMAN

2006 | RUSSELL ATHLETIC: LSU's mobile QB JaMarcus Russell had more than one way of attacking through the air, as he proved against Tennessee. | *Photograph by* BOB ROSATO

2005 | IN LIKE QUINN: Notre Dame's Brady Quinn reached out to touch paydirt and give the Irish a late but short-lived lead over USC. | *Photograph by* BILL FRAKES

A CAROLINA CHOO CHOO

BY RON FIMRITE

It has been nearly 25 years since Charlie Justice played his last game at tailback for North Carolina. He was a folk hero at the time—and be still is. —from SI, OCTOBER 15, 1973

THEY SEEM LIKE PHANTOMS, these All-America football heroes of the Forties. If we do not condemn them to a lifetime of boyhood, we speak of them as if they were long dead. "Say, whatever did happen to old Choo Choo Justice?" Choo Choo thrives, of course, and so do his contemporary deities: Georgia's Charley Trippi, Johnny Lujack (once nearly as celebrated as the Four Horse-men at Notre Dame), Southern Methodist's Doak Walker. They are very much alive, these phantoms, but they survive in times that must seem strange to them. College football today has no heroes, only superstars, and superstars are fallible; the heroes of the postwar '40s were not. They appeared at a time when a nation weary of war and Depression wanted escapist entertainment. The people had had their fill of the heroes in foxholes and the command post; they wanted them now in the backfield or the outfield.

College football would prosper in this atmosphere. It would be the game's finest hour and its last alone on the stage, for in the next decade the professionals—with their ally, television—would start to dominate. But in the years immediately follow-ing the war, the college game and the college football hero fired the public's imagination. And with rosters swollen with returning servicemen who were older, larger and more expe-rienced than their prewar predecessors, the game had never been played better.

This period would also be the last fling of the triple-threat man, the versatile player, usually a single-wing tailback, who ran, passed and kicked. The increasing sophistication of the T formation, with its emphasis on specialization, would soon render him obsolete. Justice, Walker, Trippi—even the 'T' quarterback Lujack—were all practitioners of versatility. They could dominate a game in a way no longer possible. In separate games in 1945, for example, Trippi set Southeastern Confer-ence records in rushing and passing. The triple-threater was truly responsible for his team's entire offense and was thus the object of unusual exposure. Furthermore, the four great All-Americas of this period also could play defense—and did. It was not hard to find them on a football field.

And so they were honored in their time as few athletes before or since have been. Reflecting on this, Doak Walker has said, "I suppose Charlie Justice and I got about as much publicity as any two men who ever lived." It was not an out-landish boast.

North Carolina had never been asked to a football bowl game before the arrival of Charlie Justice. In his four years there (freshmen were eligible then as now), the team went to three bowls and rejected an invitation to a fourth.

Charlie was already famous when he played in his first scrimmage for coach Carl Snavely in Chapel Hill in 1946. He had been a high school sensation in Asheville—he averaged 25 yards a carry his senior year—and he had been the star of a Bainbridge Naval Training Center team that had in its lineup experienced former college and professional players. Maybe hundreds of schools had offered him scholarships after the war, but Charlie had chosen to stay home in North Carolina. As a Tar Heel, Justice gained 5,176 yards rushing and passing from 1946 through '49. He scored 39 touchdowns and passed for 26 more. He averaged 42.5 punts on 251 punts and he re-turned 74 punts for an average of 16.2 yards per return. He was a first-team All-America in both '48 and '49. He still holds school records in total yardage, scoring and punting. But sta-tistics cannot measure his magnetism.

"Charlie came along at a time when every little kid wanted to grow up to be somebody else, a football hero or even presi-dent," says Chapel Hill publisher Orville Campbell, a close friend of Justice's. "You don't hear college kids talking that way anymore. I imagine if Charlie were to come to Carolina now and have four years like he had back then, there wouldn't be the same great love for him. But I tell you, nobody captured the imagination of the American public the way Charlie cap-tured the imagination of the people of North Carolina."

Even in this atmosphere, Charlie Justice was unique. The state of Texas had produced football heroes by the score before Walker, Lujack merely entered the Notre Dame pantheon, and before Trippi at Georgia there had never been Frankie Sink-wich. But North Carolina had never had anyone quite like the man who, in the words of a Navy officer who saw him go wild for Bainbridge in a service game, "runs just like a little old choo choo train." . . .

EVEN A loss to Rice in the 1950 Cotton Bowl, his final college game, could not tarnish Justice's dazzling career or his legend in the Tar Heel State.

1995 | ON THIS PLAY, there was no getting around BC's Mark Noti for Ohio State's Winfield Garnett in the Buckeyes' 38–6 win. | *Photograph by* DAMIAN STROHMEYER

1989 | BROWNING NAGLE of Louisville (opposite) found himself amidst of a mound of Mountaineers during a 30–21 West Virginia win. | *Photograph by* JOHN BIEVER

Political Football

Presidents, senators, generals, even a Supreme Court justice—many of our leaders got an early taste of the rough and tumble (to say nothing of teamwork and interference) on the gridiron, be it a real one or, in one celebrated instance, a reel one

BYRON R. WHITE
Supreme Court justice "Whizzer" was second in the '37 Heisman voting as a Colorado back.

EDWARD M. KENNEDY
Harvard end Teddy (88) dropped this one but tallied his team's only TD in a 21–7 loss to Yale in '55.

1912 | THE WEST POINT squad featured halfback and future president Dwight D. Eisenhower (third from left) and center Omar Bradley (far right), later to be General of the Army. | *Photograph by UPI/CORBIS*

RONALD REAGAN
In his first career, "Dutch" scored as the Gipper in 1940's Knute Rockne All American.

RICHARD M. NIXON
The youthful Dick was a scrappy scrub on the Whittier College squad in the '30s.

GERALD R. FORD
Michigan's MVP in '34, standout center "Junie" would spurn the Detroit Lions for Yale Law School.

157

SAY IT'S SO, JOE

BY TIM LAYDEN

He can't get his coach to admit it, but Penn State's brash linebacker is the best in the country. —*from* SI, AUGUST 16, 1999

PENN STATE IS A PLACE WHERE football players are expected to be gentlemen. It is a place where nominations to the *Playboy* All-America team are unwelcome and where the drab uniforms are designed as armor against ego inflation. It's also a place where emotions on the field are kept in control, lest they interfere with the blessed execution of football fundamentals and where the prescribed pecking order demands that seniors rule and underclassmen wait. If Penn State football lived and breathed, it would floss twice daily and come to a full stop before turning right on red.

Such staunch conservatism can take root when the man who sets the tone is a campus fixture for 50 years (think about that), including 33 as the coach. Joe Paterno gives the public a program it can feel good about. For this he is deified as an island of dignity, and he deserves it.

Yet occasionally there comes a player who tries to upset the Happy Valley status quo. For 1999 junior outside linebacker LaVar Arrington has volunteered to lead the latest attempt to revolutionize Penn State football. "They do things a certain way around here," says Arrington. "I don't think that's going to win you many national titles, not in 1999 or 2000. Athletes have evolved. To win a national title, you put your best athletes out there, and you let them play with emotion and intensity. You don't change them."

Arrington speaks from experience when he offers this blasphemous take on the Penn State philosophy. He came to State College as the *Parade* national high school player of the year, a 6' 3", 230-pound linebacker–running back from North Hills High in Pittsburgh. As a true freshman that year, he played some at outside linebacker. A year later he dominated preseason practices but didn't start the season opener, dues-paying that he found humiliating. "They like to give the older guys an opportunity," says Brandon Short, a senior linebacker who plays alongside Arrington. "In LaVar's case, they wanted to test his mental toughness. I said to him, 'You're the best athlete out here, no way they can keep you off the field.' But it was rough on him."

Arrington was made a starter in the second game and tore through the season as if he were trying to cram a career into 10 weekends. It wasn't just that he finished second on the team in tackles (67), and third on the team in tackles for lost yardage (17) and sacks (seven). Or that he tied for the team lead in passes broken up (11) and intercepted two others, returning one for a touchdown. It was the way he did all of those things with reckless domination. Arrington was voted the Big Ten's defensive player of the year and a first team All-America. Illinois coach Ron Turner compares him to Michael Jordan. Michigan coach Lloyd Carr compares him with Lawrence Taylor. "When you're standing on the sideline, as a coach, you just feel his presence out there," says Carr. Arrington also punctuated his play with a stylish flair. He celebrated big hits and taunted opponents. When a Michigan tackle pancaked Arrington in the first quarter of Penn State's 27–0 loss to the Wolverines, Arrington, angry that what he thought was an obvious holding penalty hadn't been called, drilled the blocker with a forearm shiver long after the whistle, incurring a 15-yard penalty and Paterno's wrath. "The referee didn't call a penalty," Arrington says, "so I called my own."

The NFL is salivating over Arrington, who will seriously consider leaving college after this season. Pro personnel people won't comment publicly on Arrington, for fear that Paterno, in retaliation, will tighten his already rigid access to Penn State practices, but this is a summary of how they feel about Arrington: an explosive hitter with a nasty streak; has a freaky build—looks gangly and not too flexible, but is nevertheless powerful; top five pick whenever he comes out; and the type of player other players will be compared with someday.

On the other hand Paterno makes the following evaluation: "He's not even our best player. He might not even be our best linebacker, behind Brandon Short and [senior] Mac Morrison. He made a few spectacular plays. He's our best athlete, and he has great potential, but that's all. People want me to say he's the best linebacker I've ever coached. Put him in the same class as Shane Conlan and Jack Ham? You've got to be kidding. Someday, he might be all those things."

There is clearly a motivational tug-of-war in progress between the 72-year-old coaching legend and a 21-year-old linebacker who is—sorry, Joe—one of the best players in school history. It isn't personal. Arrington is the only Penn State player who will walk into a team meeting and slap Paterno on the butt. "He's a good kid," Paterno says. "Lots of personality." . . .

A SUMMA cum laude product of Linebacker U., Arrington had a genius for seeking and destroying ballcarriers like Northwestern wideout D'Wayne Bates.

1991 | EVEN BACKSLIDING, the ref fixed a cold stare on Kansas DT Kyle Moore (96) as he pursued Colorado QB Vance Joseph. | *Photograph by* RICHARD MACKSON

1984 | AN INTREPID yet wide-eyed umpire ended up a little too close to the action when Purdue played host to Ohio State. | *Photograph by* MANNY MILLAN

Sammy Baugh
BACK/PUNTER
TCU 1934-36

Knute Rockne
COACH
Notre Dame 1918-30

Herschel Walker
BACK
Georgia 1980-82

John Hannah
GUARD/TACKLE
Alabama 1970-72

Ron Yary
TACKLE
USC 1965-67

Pudge Heffelfinger
GUARD
Yale 1888-91

Glenn Davis

BACK

Army 1943–46

Chuck Bednarik

CENTER/LINEBACKER

Penn 1945–48

Leon Hart

END

Notre Dame 1946–49

Orlando Pace

TACKLE

Ohio State 1994–96

Jerry Rice

END

Mississippi Valley State 1981–84

Red Grange

BACK

Illinois 1923–25

Jim Brown

BACK

Syracuse 1954–56

Big Men

On Campus

IT'S NOT AS EASY AS IT LOOKS, THIS BUSINESS OF SELECTING THE CREAM OF THE COLLEGE FOOTBALL CROP,

position by position, offense and defense and specialists, from the sport's earliest days right up to this year's BCS title game. For starters, the athletes who labored in the eras before free substitutions and platoons were playing a different game. And as if it weren't tough enough to compare players from vastly different eras, we made the job even tougher by limiting our selections to one player per school. Who, for instance, would you take from Illinois: Red Grange or Dick Butkus? Who from Alabama: Don Hutson or John Hannah or Lee Roy Jordan? Which USC tailback—if, indeed, you chose a Trojan tailback over Ronnie Lott or Ron Yary? Which Syracuse running back? Which Penn State linebacker? Do you tap Nebraska's fabled center Dave Rimington or the magical Johnny Rodgers? Fully aware of the minefield we were about to cross but nonetheless undaunted, we polled more than two dozen current and former SI football writers and editors, then tabulated their votes, argued among ourselves and made the final, painful cuts. The arguments will no doubt continue. But before considering any substitutions, feast your eyes on the group portrait painted by one of America's foremost illustrators and, only then, think about which guys you'd cut out of the picture to open up spots on a pretty fair football team.

ILLUSTRATION BY C.F. PAYNE

Hugh Green
DEFENSIVE END
Pittsburgh 1977–80

Tommy Nobis
LINEBACKER
Texas 1963–65

Deion Sanders
DEFENSIVE BACK
Florida State 1985–88

Doak Walker
BACK/KICKER
SMU 1945, '47–49

Gale Sayers
BACK/RETURNS
Kansas 1962–64

Lawrence Taylor
LINEBACKER
North Carolina 1977–80

Johnny Rodgers
RETURNS/RECEIVER
Nebraska 1970–72

Charles Woodson
DEFENSIVE BACK/RECEIVER
Michigan 1995-97

Jack Ham
LINEBACKER
Penn State 1968-70

Kenny Easley
DEFENSIVE BACK
UCLA 1977-80

Bubba Smith
DEFENSIVE END
Michigan State 1964-66

Jim Thorpe
BACK
Carlisle 1907-08, '11-12

Paul (Bear) Bryant
COACH
Alabama 1958-82

Lee Roy Selmon
DEFENSIVE TACKLE
Oklahoma 1972-75

Bronko Nagurski
TACKLE/BACK
Minnesota 1927-29

2001 | TEXAS QUARTERBACK Chris Simms was a Longhorn sandwich between Oklahoma's Cory Heinecke (89) and Jimmy Wilkerson. | *Photograph by* JOHN BIEVER

1990 | UNDER WRAPS by Spencer Hammond of Alabama, Georgia's Larry Ware had nowhere to run during the Bulldogs' 17–16 win. | *Photograph by* JOHN BIEVER

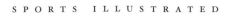

1935 | Jay Berwanger, the first Heisman winner, was one of the last leatherheads.

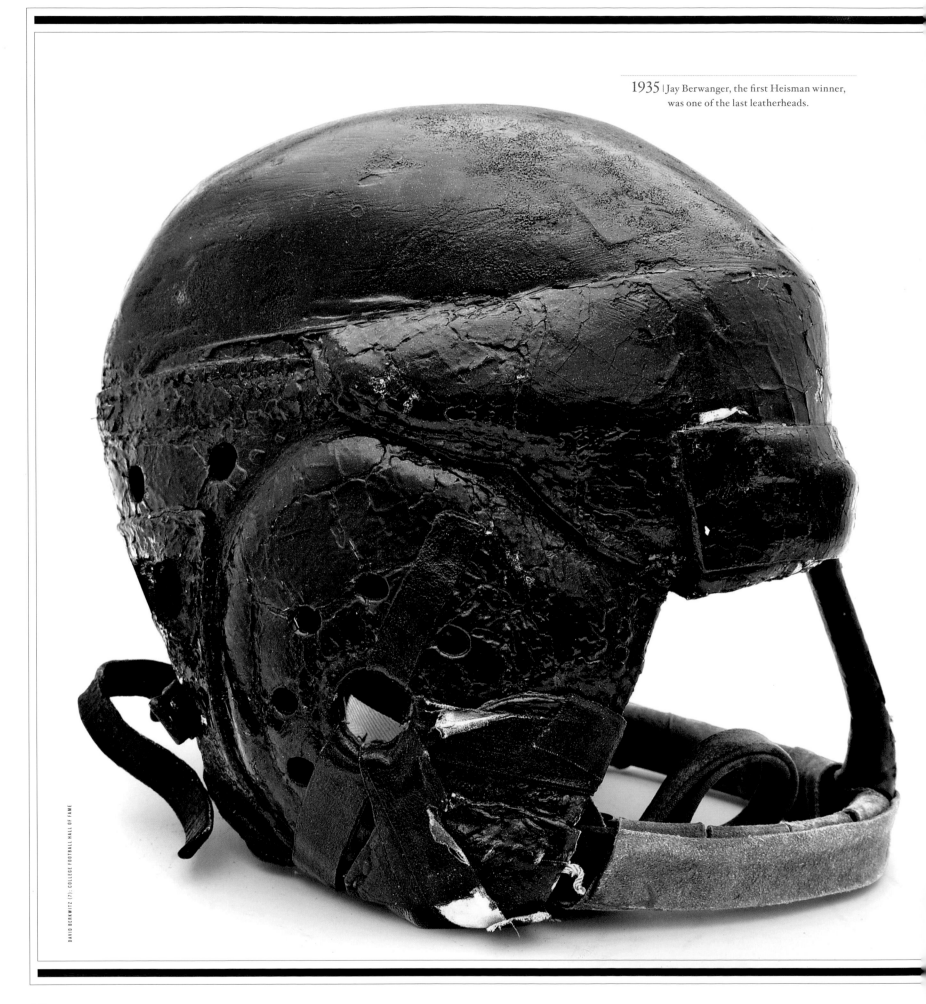

> **Artifacts**

Helmet to Helmet

Met with derision in the early 1900s, head coverings have morphed from rudimentary leather skullcaps to padded high-tech plastic shells that absorb—and, alas, deliver—some of the game's hardest blows

1895 | The harness was a feeble response to the game's ear-ripping violence.

1919 | No Buckeye leaves, but the gear of Ohio State's Chic Harley had ventilation.

1930 | Fred Sington's hat absorbed some shots aimed at the heady Alabama tackle.

1950 | Plastic guards like Notre Dame's were the face of football by mid-century.

1964 | Tulsa's tossing QB Jerry Rhome could scan the secondary over a single bar.

1999 | An uncaged Badger, Wisconsin's Ron Dayne bulled his way to the Heisman.

STEVE SUPERIOR

BY S.L. PRICE

That's what peevish rivals called Florida coach Steve Spurrier, whose arrogance—not to mention the Gators' success—kept other coaches steaming. —*from SI, OCTOBER 23, 1995*

THE VOICE CAME SLIDING DOWN out of the stands two Saturdays ago, a bayou twang thickened by liquor and envy and fury at the God who would foist such a man upon the rest of us. "You're lucky, Spurrier! You ain't that good!" But the Florida football coach couldn't hear; Steve Spurrier stood watching his undefeated team finish its calm dismissal of Louisiana State for the eighth straight time, watching from the sidelines as his Gators gave the lie to LSU's faith in its once awesome home field advantage. He was too far away, and when the voice came down again, it had lost something. "You're lucky . . . " it said, and then there was just this insecure silence, because that's not true and everyone knows, and that's what's so galling. Look at him! He's tall, lean and, at 50, still has his hair, and, damn it, he nails his putts and has a Heisman Trophy and a 29-year marriage and loyal children and . . . . You ain't that good!

They hate him. At Auburn they hate him for his crack last year about the Tigers' soft schedule and, even more, for Florida's frightfully casual 49–38 dismissal last Saturday of Auburn's national-title hopes. At Georgia they still talk about the time Bulldog coach Ray Goff, tired of Spurrier's yapping, reportedly growled that he would like to get Spurrier alone in an alley for 30 minutes. At North Carolina they still haven't forgotten how he quite happily pushed his 1988 Duke team, which led 34–0, to humiliate the Tar Heels with another score. As his former coach, colleague and opponent Pepper Rodgers once put it, "Embarrassment is part of the game to him."

Spurrier can be smug and mean, generous and warm, and with friends and enemies alike he has a free and deadly tongue. He possesses the dubious talent of sensing someone's weak spot and striking, such as the time at a coaches' gathering in Hawaii when Spurrier needled then Volunteers coach Johnny Majors about a loss to Alabama the previous fall, provoking a red-faced screaming match. "He *will* express himself—I'll leave it at that," says Majors, who's now at Pitt.

But at Florida State they may hate him most, because

though Spurrier has beaten the Seminoles just once in the five-plus seasons he has been at Florida, two summers ago he unerringly heckled the players involved in their notorious Foot Locker buying spree by calling their school Free Shoes University. Then, just to make sure everyone got his point, Spurrier refused to recant; instead he wondered out loud about the shine on all those new cars in the Florida State player parking lot. "I'm not saying anybody broke any rules; I'm just saying there was a feeling of, well, those kids are driving awfully nice cars," Spurrier says innocently. "How's it happen?"

Mostly, though, they loathe Spurrier in all those Southern towns because the Gators have, after 56 years of nothing, won three SEC championships since he came back to Florida, and he's the reason why. Under Spurrier the Gators have gone 55-12-1 and have become a perennial Top 10 power.

Worse, Spurrier has gone about winning without engaging in the time-honored Bear Bryant style of mushing words into meaningless clichés; he pretends no modesty. "I don't look at him as overly arrogant," says Terry Dean, the former Gators quarterback whose benching last season led to a bitter and public rupture with Spurrier. "Maybe egomaniacal." Steve Superior was how legendary Auburn coach Shug Jordan pronounced Spurrier's name when Spurrier was a Heisman-winning quarterback for Florida in the mid-1960s, and now that name is said with a sneer.

"Arrogant . . . cocky . . . loudmouth—well, what else could they say?" Spurrier says, voice rising into his oft-imitated squawk. "Teams are not supposed to like their opponents if the opponents are beatin' them. And I am a little different. I read something once that I think is so true: If you want to be successful, you have to do it the way everybody does it and do it a lot better--or you have to do it differently. I can't outwork anybody and I can't coach the off-tackle play better than anybody else. So I figured I'd try to coach some different ball plays, and instead of poor-mouthing my team, I'd try to build it up to the point where the players think, Coach believes we're pretty good; by golly, let's go prove it."

"I can't make star players out of all of 'em," Spurrier says with a shrug, and, no, he doesn't care how that makes him sound. Once, while at Duke in the late 1980s, Spurrier telephoned a writer at a local newspaper and requested that he not be referred to as an "offensive genius." Asked what he would prefer, Spurrier said, "I don't know. How 'bout . . . 'mastermind'? " . . .

HARDLY HUMBLE in '66, Spurrier had headlines, a wife (Jerri) and soon a Heisman, but his coaching genius would make the fame of this Gator even greater.

1937 | LOOKING FOR running room against Columbia, Stanford's Peter Fay (34) keyed off a teammate's block on John Siegal (28), but the Indians (later to be the Cardinal) were held to a scoreless tie by the team that had upset them in the '34 Rose Bowl. | *Photograph by* BROWN BROTHERS

1955 | **ARMY'S PLATOON** took the Michie Stadium field behind All-America end Don Holleder (16), who would die in Vietnam in '67. | *Photograph by* RICHARD MEEK

1968 | **RALLYING AROUND** sophomore quarterback Joe Theismann, Notre Dame pulled out a 21–21 tie against unbeaten Southern Cal. | *Photograph by* SHEEDY & LONG

ALL THE WAY
WITH O.J.

BY DAN JENKINS

The game of the year, and very likely the national championship, went to USC when its peerless runner with aching feet finally outshone UCLA's matchless quarterback and his aching ribs.

—from SI, NOVEMBER 27, 1967

HERE IS THE WAY IT WAS in that college football game last week for the championship of the earth, Saturn, Pluto and Los Angeles: UCLA's Gary Beban had a rib cage that looked like an abstract painting in purples and pinks, and USC's O.J. Simpson had a foot that looked like it belonged in a museum of natural history, but they kept getting up from these knockout blows, gasping, coming back, and doing all of their outrageously heroic things. So, do you know what? In the end, the difference in the biggest game of the 1967 season and one of the best since the ears of helmets stopped flapping was that this guy with a name like a Russian poet, Zenon Andrusyshyn, couldn't place-kick the ball over this other guy with a name like the president of the Van Nuys Jaycees—Bill Hayhoe. And that was the contest. Andrusyshyn would try to side-boot a field goal or extra point for UCLA, and Hayhoe, who happens to be 6' 8", would raise up. The ball would go splat, plink or karang. The last time Hayhoe did it, he tipped the leather just enough to make the Bruins fail on a precious conversion and USC got away with a 21–20 victory in a spectacle that will surely be remembered for ages, or at least as long as German-born, Ukrainian, Canadian-bred soccer-style kickers play the game.

Of course it is not exactly fair to insinuate that Zenon Andrusyshyn, the German-Ukrainian-Canadian, was the goat of the whole desperate afternoon. Though only a sophomore, he is a splendid kicker who boomed punts into the California heavens all day. Rather, it is more accurate to give credit to USC's John McKay for one of those little coaching touches that sometimes supplies a subtle edge. This time it proved to be a subtle edge that gave McKay the most important game of this life.

"We knew he kicked it low, so we just put the tallest guy we had in there on defense," said McKay later, in what may have been the happiest dressing room since showers were invented. "We told the kids it wasn't so important that they bust through and make him rush the kicks as it was just getting to the scrimmage line and raising their arms high."

In his wry, twinkling way, McKay then lit a cigar and said, "I call that brilliant coaching."

Everything about the day was brilliant, of course—as more than 90,000 limp souls in the Los Angeles Memorial Coliseum certainly noted, and as millions of others watching on national television must have too. Led by those folklore characters, Gary Beban and O.J. Simpson, both teams played extremely well, considering the slightly barbaric circumstances. Not only was the national championship quite possibly at stake, but so were a few other odds and ends, such as the Rose Bowl bid, the Pacific Eight title, the Heisman Trophy, some All-America trinkets and a couple of coaching reputations. That both squads and staffs went into the gnawing pressure of this kind of Saturday with such poise was unique enough. But that they also managed to litter the premises with so much brilliant play was downright against the rules for games of the century, era, decade, year (choose one).

Some of the big stakes in the game were indeed decided by that one-point margin, which is growing fatter by the hour. USC's 9–1 record measured against the quality of its schedule makes the Trojans the most deserving team for all the No. 1 cups and saucers. Some things obviously were not settled last Saturday, however, like, for instance, the individual duel between UCLA's Beban and USC's Simpson.

Although neither player was 100% physically, both were superb in clutch after clutch. While he practically had to crawl to the sideline no less than five times to regain his breath because of his injured ribs, Beban whirled the Bruins to three touchdowns, passing for more than 300 yards.

Meanwhile, Simpson, his right foot throbbing inside a shoe with a special sponge cover, wearily hobbled away from piles of brutal tacklers and eventually managed to race for a total of 177 yards and two touchdowns.

Had the Heisman Trophy award, therefore, really been decided by a couple of young men named Zenon Andrusyshyn and Bill Hayhoe? As Jim Murray of the *Los Angeles Times* said, "They should send the Heisman out here with two straws." . . .

THE LIGHT was shining on Simpson, whose 64-yard fourth-quarter touchdown dash burned the Bruins and their eventual Heisman winner Beban.

1955 | YALE BACKS (from left) Gene Coker, Dennis McGill, Dean Loucks and Al Ward weren't afraid to get a little dirt under their fingernails—or anywhere else—during their 7–2 season. | *Photograph by* JERRY COOKE

> THE ALL-DECADE TEAM

OFFENSE

E	*Mike Ditka*	PITTSBURGH
E	*Howard Twilley*	TULSA
T	*Ron Yary*	USC
T	*Bobby Bell*	MINNESOTA
G	*Bob Brown*	NEBRASKA
G	*Rick Redman*	WASHINGTON
C	*Lee Roy Jordan*	ALABAMA
B	*Roger Staubach*	NAVY
B	*Gale Sayers*	KANSAS
B	*O.J. Simpson*	USC
B	*Ernie Davis*	SYRACUSE

DEFENSE

DL	*Ted Hendricks*	MIAMI
DL	*Bubba Smith*	MICHIGAN STATE
DL	*Mike Reid*	PENN STATE
DL	*Joe Greene*	NORTH TEXAS
LB	*Tommy Nobis*	TEXAS
LB	*Dick Butkus*	ILLINOIS
LB	*Steve Kiner*	TENNESSEE
DB	*Jerry Stovall*	LSU
DB	*Johnny Roland*	MISSOURI
DB	*George Webster*	MICHIGAN STATE
DB	*Tom Curtis*	MICHIGAN

> NICKNAMES <

Lance [Bambi] Alworth ∧
Donny [The Golden Palomino] Anderson
Terry [The Blond Bomber] Bradshaw
Bob [The Boomer] Brown
Junious [Buck] Buchanan
Don [Air] Coryell
[Iron] Mike Ditka
Carl [Moose] Eller
[Mean] Joe Greene
Ted [The Mad Stork] Hendricks
David [Deacon] Jones
Willie [Honey Bear] Lanier
[Wonderful] Willie Richardson
James [Rabbit] Saxton
Glenn [Bo] Schembechler
Ron [Jingle Joints] Sellers
O.J [The Juice] Simpson
Charles [Bubba] Smith
Roger [The Dodger] Staubach
Jack [The Assassin] Tatum
Ed [The Goose] White

	HEISMAN TROPHY WINNER	RUSHING LEADER	YARDS	PASSING LEADER	YARDS
'60	JOE BELLINO Navy	BOB GAITERS New Mexico State	1,338	HAROLD STEPHENS Hardin-Simmons	1,254
'61	ERNIE DAVIS Syracuse	JIM PILOT New Mexico State	1,278	CHON GALLEGOS San Jose State	1,480
'62	TERRY BAKER Oregon State	JIM PILOT New Mexico State	1,247	DON TRULL Baylor	1,627
'63	ROGER STAUBACH Navy	DAVE CASINELLI Memphis State	1,016	DON TRULL Baylor	2,157
'64	JOHN HUARTE Notre Dame	BRIAN PICCOLO Wake Forest	1,044	JERRY RHOME Tulsa	2,870
'65	MIKE GARRETT USC	MIKE GARRETT USC	1,440	BILL ANDERSON Tulsa	3,464
'66	STEVE SPURRIER Florida	RAY McDONALD Idaho	1,329	JOHN ECKMAN Wichita State	2,339
'67	GARY BEBAN UCLA	O.J. SIMPSON USC	1,415	TERRY STONE New Mexico	1,946
'68	O.J. SIMPSON USC	O.J. SIMPSON USC	1,709	CHUCK HIXSON SMU	3,103
'69	STEVE OWENS Oklahoma	STEVE OWENS Oklahoma	1,523	JOHN REAVES Florida	2,896

>> THE DECADE'S DYNASTIES

Alabama >
From Lee Roy Jordan to Joe Namath to Ray Perkins to Kenny Stabler, stars fell on Alabama. Molded by Bear Bryant, the Crimson Tide won three national titles (1961, '64 and '65), went undefeated twice and lost once at home all decade.

USC
The modern-day Trojan dynasty began in 1962 with a national championship and produced six Top 10 finishes and another title in '67. John McKay's formula was irresistible: a mighty offensive line (with tackles like Ron Yary) leading breakaway tailbacks, among them Heisman winners Mike Garrett ('65) and O.J. Simpson ('68).

Texas
After falling just short of a national title in 1961 and '62, the Longhorns broke through in '63. Darrell Royal would win another, in '69, after six seasons with no more than one loss, an era marked by the smashing play of linebacker Tommy Nobis.

Ole Miss
The Rebels rolled early, ticking off two unbeaten seasons. Johnny Vaught's teams went to a bowl every year, winning the Sugar after the '60, '62 and '69 seasons, when their quarterback was Archie Manning, the best player and largest legend in school history.

Ohio State
Woody Hayes's Buckeyes were 8-0-1 in 1961 but were denied a possible national title when they declined a Rose Bowl bid. Seven years later, sophomores Rex Kern, Jim Stillwagon and Jack Tatum dotted the *i* with a 10–0 season, a Rose Bowl win over USC and a national championship.

A fleet of frisky backs like Mike Fracchia (30) had the Bear and 'Bama flying high.

> EPIC GAMES

< Michigan State *vs.* Notre Dame
November 19, 1966

Matching the No. 1 Irish and the No. 2 Spartans at East Lansing, the decade's most hyped battle left everyone fit to be tied. With the score 10–10 and 1:10 remaining, Notre Dame coach Ara Parseghian ordered his team to run out the clock. Though his strategy was scorned, it preserved the Irish's top ranking and national championship.

USC *vs.* UCLA
November 18, 1967

With bragging rights to L.A., the Pac-8 title, a trip to the Rose Bowl and a Heisman on the line, Trojans RB O.J. Simpson and Bruins QB Gary Beban put on an Oscar-worthy show. O.J. supplied the Hollywood ending with a 64-yard TD run, and Rikki Aldridge's extra point was the difference in the 21–20 win; Beban settled for the Heisman.

Texas vs. Arkansas
December 6, 1969

The teams came to Fayetteville with the Longhorns ranked No. 1 and the Razorbacks No. 2. In the fourth quarter, QB James Street rallied Texas from a 14–0 deficit, hitting RB Randy Peschel with a 44-yard pass on fourth-and-three to set up the tying score. Happy Feller booted the extra point to give the Horns a 15–14 victory and a Cotton Bowl berth.

> CAMPUS CULTURE

YOU'VE GOT TO...

READ IT: *The Electric Kool-Aid Acid Test*, Tom Wolfe; *To Kill a Mockingbird*, Harper Lee; *Portnoy's Complaint*, Philip Roth; *Understanding Media*, Marshall McLuhan; *Slaughterhouse-Five*, Kurt Vonnegut; *In Cold Blood*, Truman Capote; *Catch-22*, Joseph Heller; *The Best and the Brightest*, David Halberstam

HEAR IT: Bob Dylan, The Beatles, The Doors, The Rolling Stones, Jimi Hendrix, Janis Joplin, Cream, Beach Boys, Grateful Dead, Jefferson Airplane, Marvin Gaye, The Supremes, Led Zeppelin, The Who

DEAL WITH IT: Assassinations of JFK, RFK and MLK; campus protests; the draft; race riots

SEE IT: *Rowan & Martin's Laugh-In*, *The Graduate*, *Bonnie and Clyde*,

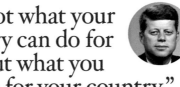

"Ask not what your country can do for you, but what you can do for your country."

—President John F. Kennedy in his inaugural address, Jan. 20, 1961

2001: A Space Odyssey, *The Tonight Show Starring Johnny Carson*, *Butch Cassidy and the Sundance Kid*, *Easy Rider*, *Midnight Cowboy*, *The Pink Panther*, *Batman*, *Star Trek*, *The Smothers Brothers*, *The Twilight Zone*

DISCUSS IT: Kennedy-Nixon debates, Apollo moon mission, civil rights, Woodstock, Maris and Mantle, women's lib, Clay/Ali, Fellini, Malcolm X, the Super Bowl

HAVE IT: Skateboard, stereo, TV dinners, zig-zags, Tang, Super Ball, color TV, McDonald's, *Rolling Stone*, touch-tone phone

WEAR IT: Long hair, tie dye, bell bottoms, miniskirts, go-go boots, Madras, granny glasses

DO IT: The Twist, "Tune in, turn on, drop out," call 911, Peace Corps, Frisbee, "Make Love, Not War"

> SMARTEST GUY IN THE WORLD

ROBERT NOYCE The founder of Fairchild Semiconductor and Intel co-invented the integrated circuit, or microchip—the seed of the computer revolution.

Signs of the times: Protest was in the air, as was the aroma of assorted illegal substances.

> BY THE NUMBERS

98.1 Extra-point percentage for Cornell's Pete Gogolak, football's first soccer-style placekicker, who went 54 for 55 from 1961 through '63.

5 Consecutive seasons (1962 to '66) that Tulsa led the nation in passing offense.

31 Tackles made by Alabama's Lee Roy Jordan in the Crimson Tide's 17–0 win over Oklahoma in the 1963 Orange Bowl.

1 Seasons (1968) that Harvard offensive guard Tom Jones—later known in Hollywood as Tommy Lee Jones—was named to the All-Ivy League first team.

102 Age of Amos Alonzo Stagg when he died on St. Patrick's Day 1965.

7 Games in which brothers Bump Elliott of Michigan and Pete Elliott of Illinois faced each other as coaches from 1960 to '66, with Bump winning six.

14 Interceptions (in 10 games) by Washington's Al Worley in 1968, the NCAA Division I record.

INNOVATOR

Emory Bellard The Texas offensive coordinator dreamed up the wishbone, a devastating option attack named for the shape in which the three running backs line up. As the Longhorns won 30 straight, from 1968 through '70, the 'bone became the rage.

1992 | STRAIN THOUGH he might, Lycoming tailback Cory Sheridan could not break the bounds of a Susquehanna gang tackle. | *Photograph by* JOHN IACONO

1991 | ILLINOIS AND Shawn Wax got whacked upside the head by Clemson and Robert O'Neal in the Tigers' 30–0 Hall of Fame Bowl win. | *Photograph by* TOM LYNN

1974 | ALABAMA'S WIZARD, Ozzie Newsome became the Tide's greatest tight end ever in part by applying elbow grease. | *Photograph by* PAUL W. BRYANT MUSEUM

1954 | USC'S JAGUAR, Jon Arnett was known for his breakaway runs but also proved to be quite a grabber during a 29–27 win over Cal. | *Photograph by* PHIL BATH

MR. INSIDE & MR. OUTSIDE

BY RON FIMRITE

The fabled Army teams of the 1940s could launch a full frontal attack with Doc Blanchard or outflank opponents with the fleet-footed Glenn Davis. —*from* SI, NOVEMBER 21, 1988

BLANCHARD AND DAVIS. THEY are as different as two men can be, and yet it is almost impossible for those who remember them to say one name without the other. They are the Damon and Pythias, the Chang and Eng, the MacNeil and Lehrer of football. Indeed, though they rarely see each other anymore and live many miles apart, though they have followed entirely separate paths since they left West Point more than 41 years ago and were never really that close, Doc Blanchard and Glenn Davis are destined to march in lockstep through time. They will forever be what George Trevor of the old New York *Sun* called them long ago in a moment of matchless inspiration, Mr. Inside and Mr. Outside.

They were running backs who perfectly complemented each other: the one, Blanchard, a battering ram up the middle; the other, Davis, a wraith around end. Together they formed the most devastating backfield combination since the Four Horsemen of Notre Dame 20 years earlier. Individually, they rank among the finest backs ever to play college football. Their coach, Col. Earl (Red) Blaik, said, "There is no comparing them with anyone else. They were the best."

Blanchard and Davis were consensus All-Americas in 1944, '45 and '46, the only three-time All-America backfield teammates. They won the Heisman Trophy in successive years, Blanchard in '45, Davis in '46. Their skills were hardly defined by their sobriquets. Mr. Inside had the speed to run outside, and he frequently did. Indeed, Blanchard ran 100 yards in under 10 seconds. He also punted, kicked off and occasionally kicked extra points. On defense (Mr. Inside and Mr. Outside were two-way players), he was a punishing tackler as a linebacker. Blanchard became the first football player to win the Sullivan Award as the nation's finest amateur athlete. He dabbled in track and field his senior year and, with no previous experience in the event, was putting the shot close to

54 feet at a time when the world record was not yet 60 feet.

Blanchard was a superior athlete. Davis was an amazing one. In his four years at West Point, Davis won 10 letters: four in football, three in baseball, two in track and one in basketball. His career batting average on the Army baseball team was .403 for 51 games, and he stole 64 bases in 65 attempts. Davis may well have been the fastest football player ever to play the game up to his time. The qualifier is necessary because no one could ever be certain just how fast he was; like Blanchard, he considered track a mere diversion. But in 1947 Davis did beat Barney Ewell, the silver medalist at 100 meters in the 1948 Olympic Games, in a 6.1 60-yard dash in a meet at Madison Square Garden.

But Davis had more than speed on the football field. He was only 5' 9" and 170 pounds, but he ran with unusual power and was one of the shiftiest backs the game has ever known. "He and Doc were both easy to block for," says DeWitt (Tex) Coulter, an All-America tackle on the Blanchard-Davis teams. "You didn't really need to get in a solid lick, because they had this sense of where to go, that great running instinct."

Davis still holds or shares five NCAA rushing and scoring records. His career-average gain of 8.26 yards (2,957 yards in 358 carries) has been the standard for 42 years. Together, Davis and Blanchard hold the career record for most touchdowns and points scored by two players on the same team—97 and 585, respectively. Granted, some of those extraordinary numbers were achieved against weak wartime opponents, but by 1946 the big boys were back. Mr. Inside and Mr. Outside were equal to the occasion.

"I finally figured out what will stop Blanchard and Davis," New York Giants coach Steve Owen slyly advised some of his college coaching friends. "Graduation."

And so it did. Blanchard graduated 296th and Davis 305th in a 1947 class of 310, but the Corps of Cadets gave each of them the longest and loudest cheers heard that day. Actually, there was rejoicing all over the country in that second postwar spring. The boys were home again, wartime restrictions had been lifted, and the nation was entering an era of unprecedented prosperity. But at the same time that veterans were shedding their uniforms for civilian clothes, the two most famous football players in the land were getting their marching orders . . . .

THE DASHING Davis (41) won the '46 Heisman in Army's double-barreled backfield, aiming at foes' flanks when Blanchard wasn't blasting up the middle.

2006 | GEORGIA TECH'S Biletnikoff Award–winning wideout Calvin Johnson flashed his skills with seven catches against Notre Dame. | *Photograph by* BOB ROSATO

1997 | TIP-TOEING PAST Tori Noel, Florida's All-America receiver Jacquez Green helped the Gators hand Tennessee its only regular-season loss. | *Photograph by* BILL FRAKES

from FRESH BREEZES THROUGH A MAUSOLEUM

BY DAN JENKINS | *SI, October 9, 1972*

S OMEWHERE BACK IN THE HISTORY OF
college football there was a stereotyped coach, complete with growl,
baggy canvas pants, baseball cap and whistle around the neck who
conjured up the myth that freshmen cannot play varsity ball because
they are inexperienced and undeveloped. Innocently, the world has
lived with that myth for quite a while, without questioning it, except during the
periods of the Second World War and the Korean involvement. Freshmen cannot
play. Not ready yet. That's it.

Well, here we all now sit in Ohio Stadium, all 86,000 of us, right here on the banks
of Woody Hayes's Olentangy River in Columbus, in utter and complete shock at the
whirling, dashing sight of 18-year-old Archie Griffin, freshman tailback, three days
in classes at Ohio State, who has just ripped off a record 239 yards. Archie Griffin
has just spun off wicked runs of 55 yards and 32 yards and 22 yards and 20 yards and
11 yards and assorted runs of six and eight and nine yards. He has sneaked through
tiny little holes in the line, and he has slid outside and tiptoed down sidelines. He has
bumped into people from North Carolina and knocked them down. He has burst
into the sunlight of the secondary and darted this way and that. He has scored a
touchdown and set up other touchdowns and a field goal and won a game for the
Buckeyes, the final score being 29–14.

This is essentially a fullback's ballpark. Ohio Stadium belongs to those fellows from
Hayes's past who run the Robust-T and who send thunder into the minds of visitors.
But into this fullback's paradise, and in front of the roaring crowd, came this teenager
to break a 27-year-old Buckeye rushing record with astonishing ease, and break the
Tar Heels along with it. As North Carolina's Bill Dooley said afterward, "We came
here not even knowing Archie Griffin existed, and now you tell me he's a freshman!"

Archie didn't get into the game until Ohio State trailed by 7–0, and until starting
tailback Morris Bradshaw had shown he could not gain yardage. Archie, who is 5' 10"
and weighs 185, came in, an insignificant number 45 on your program, a tailback in
the Power-I that Woody runs when he isn't in the Robust-T.

Griffin was most likely a happy surprise to Hayes himself. "We've got more
depth and more potential than we've ever had," Woody said a couple of days before
North Carolina showed up. He went all through the depth that he had, and guess
what? He never even mentioned Archie Griffin. But why should he? We all know
you cannot depend on a freshman . . . .

1974 | BARRELING TOWARD his first Heisman, Griffin picked up 111 yards in a 12–10 win over
Michigan that sent the Buckeyes to their third straight Rose Bowl. | *Photograph by* WALTER IOOSS JR.

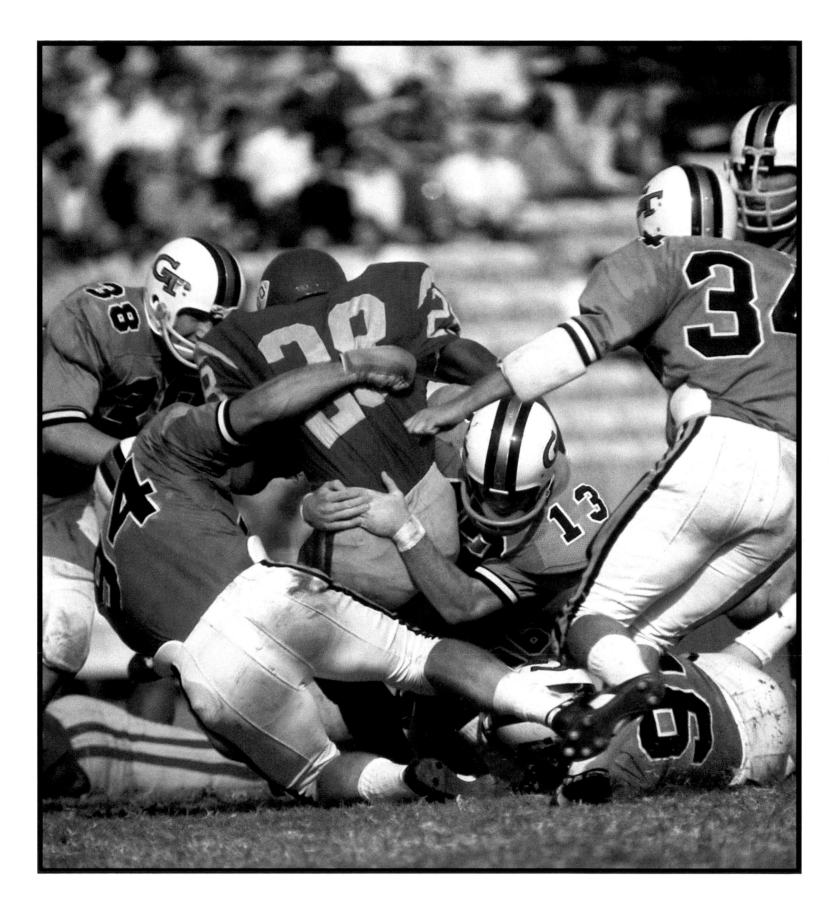

1969 | IT TOOK a swarm of Yellow Jackets to stop Southern Cal tailback Clarence Davis during the Trojans' 29–18 victory over Georgia Tech. | *Photograph by* SHEEDY & LONG

2007 | PEEKING DUCK Andre Crenshaw proved a tasty target for Kevin Brown (75) and Bruce Davis (44) when UCLA beat Oregon 16–0. | *Photograph by* DUSTIN SNIPES

A GOOD JOE

BY RICK REILLY

Joe Paterno was celebrated by SI for proving throughout his career that a teacher could be a winner too.

—*from* SI, DECEMBER 22–29, 1986

AS THIS YEAR'S SPORTSMAN OF the Year, we choose a tenured professor who wears glasses thicker than storm windows, a jacket and tie, white socks and pants legs that indicate continual fear of flash floods. He goes about 5' 10", 165 and looks less like a football coach than a CPA for an olive oil firm. On most mornings he leaves a red Ford Tempo in the modest driveway of the modest house he has owned since 1969 and walks to the office. He has worked at the same place for 37 years. For excitement he likes to sit in his La-Z-Boy and doodle on a yellow sketch pad. Such a glitzy celebrity is our honoree that his number is in the phone book.

But legends have a confounding habit of showing up in strange shapes. And a funny thing happens when this one starts to say something. Two-hundred-eighty-pound linemen, college presidents, NCAA honchos, network biggies and even your basic U.S. vice presidents cross-body-block one another to get near him. Good thing, too, because Joe Paterno, the football coach at Penn State, can teach you some of the damnedest things.

From whom else but Paterno did we learn that you can have 20/20,000 vision and still see more clearly than almost everybody else, that you can look like Bartleby but coach like Bryant, that you can have your kids hit holes like 'Bama's and books like Brown's, that the words "college" and "football" don't have to be mutually exclusive. "We try to remember," Paterno once told *The Reader's Digest*, "football is part of life —not life itself."

Maybe for that wisdom alone, we choose Paterno as Sportsman of the Year. But that's not exactly right. Because what he has done in 1986 is not much different from what he has done for 21 years. He went undefeated for the regular season. He has done that six times, a feat equaled only by Bear Bryant and Frank Leahy. In two weeks Penn State will play for the national championship. It has done that four times in the last nine years, more than any other school. Over the past two years, his team has been 22–1. But he has done better than that. From '67 to '70 he had a 31-game unbeaten streak. This year 100% of his seniors are expected to graduate. Next year Paterno will become the first Division I-A coach to achieve this trifecta: 200 victories, a winning percentage of more than .800 and an 80% graduation rate by his players. Not bad for a kid from Flatbush.

In an era of college football in which it seems everybody's hand is either in the till or balled up in a fist, Paterno sticks out like a clean thumb. And we need the guy in the Photogray trifocals more than ever. Over the last three decades, nobody has stayed truer to the game and truer to himself than Joseph Vincent Paterno, JoePa to Penn State worshippers—a man so patently stubborn that he refuses to give up on the notion that if you hack away at enough windmills, a few of the suckers will fall. Maybe we choose Paterno because he is a great football coach. Eighteen times he has finished in the Top 20, 15 times in the Top 10. Do you realize Paterno had three unbeaten teams that were voted out of national championships before he was voted into one, in 1982?

Then again, maybe we pick Paterno because he aspires to be more than a coach. Indeed, he was bred for more. Paterno's aunt was in charge of foreign languages for a Long Island school district, his cousin became president of Chrysler, his father never read the newspaper without a dictionary next to him. "At the dinner table, we were allowed to argue about anything," recalls Paterno. "And we did. Kids from the neighborhood would walk into our kitchen, unannounced, and sit in, just to listen."

To Paterno, an education was a weapon, a reward. Joey may have grown up in the same neighborhood as Vince Lombardi, but he aspired to be Clarence Darrow. In fact when Paterno accepted Rip Engle's offer right out of Brown to take an assistant coaching job at Penn State in 1950, he promised his father he did it only to earn extra money for law school. Thirty-seven years later, it looks as though Joey will never become a lawyer. He seems to have spent a lifetime making up for it.

When he won the national championship in 1982, he marched into a meeting of the university's board of trustees and, in effect, scolded them. He urged the board to raise entrance requirements and to spend more money on the library. To professors across the land, that may look like a misprint. The football coach wants to make the entrance requirements tougher? It may go down as the only time in history that a coach yearned for a school its football team could be proud of . . . .

PATERNO'S METHODS and values, like his teams' uniforms, are old-fashioned and unadorned, yet he would remain conspicuously successful even into his 80s.

1968 | THE NEWFANGLED wishbone suited Texas runner Steve (Big Woo) Worster
to a T during the Longhorns' 35–14 pasting of Texas A & M. | *Photograph by* HY PESKIN

1993 | OTTO THE ORANGE was full of Syracuse cheer when his team beat Colorado in the Fiesta Bowl on New Year's Day. | *Photograph by* SYRACUSE UNIVERSITY

1920s | COLUMBIA'S LION roared for players like fullback Lou Gehrig on South Field at the school's campus in upper Manhattan. | *Photograph by* BROWN BROTHERS

CUT OFF FROM THE HERD

BY S.L. PRICE

Randy Moss led the revitalization of Marshall's football program, but he cared little about its past—and would not be around for its future. —*from* SI, AUGUST 25, 1997

EVERYBODY'S WATCHING HIM. Randy Moss can feel the eyes of the lunchtime crowd at the Bob Evans restaurant, the double takes and furtive glances from the men in short sleeves and wide ties. He's got his act down: gray hood over his head, butt slumped in the booth, eyes as lifeless as buttons. Moss is a wide receiver at Marshall University, in Huntington, W.Va., and he figures to be rich before long. He jabs at his toast with a plastic straw. "If I didn't have this hood on, and they saw us sitting here, people would say an agent picked up Randy Moss and took him to Bob Evans," he says. "That's why I got this hood on. Some know I'm here and you're here, they see a bill and they'll say, 'The agent paid for his food.' Anything can happen."

He shrugs. Moss says he doesn't care about the world's judgments anymore, and it's easy to believe he means it. Certainly no player in college football bears more stains on his name. Two and a half years ago, as a high school senior, Moss stomped a kid in a fight, pleaded guilty to two counts of battery and was sentenced to 30 days in jail and a year's probation. That cost him a scholarship to Notre Dame. He enrolled at Florida State. The following spring he broke probation by smoking marijuana, was kicked out of school and served two more months in prison. Then last fall, as Moss was on his way to shattering various NCAA and Marshall records with 28 touchdowns and 1,709 receiving yards as a freshman, he was charged with domestic battery against the mother of his baby daughter.

Yet Moss is not much interested in image-mending. His hair is braided in long rows against his skull. "People perceive: Only black thug guys have braids," he says, his voice carrying to a dozen tables. "They perceive me as a thug? I'm not. I'm a gentleman. I know what I am, my mom knows what I am. Don't judge me until you know me."

Notre Dame did just that, and Moss will never forgive the school for it. "They didn't take me, because they see me as a thug," he says. "Then Florida State . . . I don't know. You win some, you lose some. That's a loss." Moss pauses, laughs a humorless laugh. "But in the long run I'm going to have the victory. In the long run . . . victorious."

Moss is sure of this because he has sports' trump card: talent. Better, Moss has the kind of breathtaking athletic gifts seen once in a generation. At 6' 5", with a 39-inch vertical leap and 4.25 speed in the 40, he established himself as West Virginia's greatest high school athlete since Jerry West. Irish coach Lou Holtz declared him one of the best high school football players he'd ever seen. Nearly every college wanted him, troubled or not. During Moss's trial for the stomping incident, Kanawha County prosecutor Bill Forbes received a half-dozen calls from football coaches around the country assuring him they could make Moss a better citizen if he was released to their care. Florida State coach Bobby Bowden ultimately got Moss and quickly understood his colleagues' hunger. Early in the fall of 1995, during an impromptu late-night footrace among the Seminoles' fastest players, Moss came in second. When he went through practice the following spring as a redshirt freshman, the defense couldn't stop him from scoring. "He was as good as Deion Sanders," Bowden says. "Deion's my measuring stick for athletic ability, and this kid was just a bigger Deion."

Marshall took Moss in last summer after his chances elsewhere had dwindled to nothing, and he was instantly recognized as the best player on the practice field. He then strolled through Marshall's Southern Conference schedule like a grown man dropped into Pop Warner games. His teammates called him the Freak. In the Division I-AA title game, a 49–29 rout of Montana, Moss caught four touchdown passes to tie the single-season college record of 28 set by Jerry Rice in 1984 as a senior.

Before coming to Marshall last year, football coach Bobby Pruett spent two years as defensive coordinator at Florida watching dominant Gators wideouts such as Ike Hilliard and Reidel Anthony, who went seventh and 16th, respectively, in the first round of the 1997 NFL draft. Neither, Pruett says, had Moss's weaponry. "He's the best athlete I've ever been around," Pruett says . . . .

TDS AND TROUBLE were both common for the hugely talented Moss, who toyed with overmatched opponents, reaching paydirt 53 times in two years at Marshall.

1999 | PENN STATE'S David Macklin (27) and Derek Fox held onto Minnesota's Ron Johnson, who still held on for a touchdown catch. | *Photograph by* AL TIELEMANS

1993 | CARLOS YANCY of Georgia had a tight rein—maybe too tight—on Willie Jackson, but Florida made the bigger splash in a 33–26 win. | *Photograph by* AL TIELEMANS

THE 1970s

> THE ALL-DECADE TEAM

OFFENSE		
TE	**Ken MacAfee**	NOTRE DAME
OL	**Brad Budde**	USC
OL	**John Hannah**	ALABAMA
OL	**Jerry Sisemore**	TEXAS
OL	**John Hicks**	OHIO STATE
C	**Jim Ritcher**	NC STATE
WR	**Lynn Swann**	USC
QB	**Jim Plunkett**	STANFORD
RB	**Billy Sims**	OKLAHOMA
RB	**Archie Griffin**	OHIO STATE
RB	**Johnny Rodgers**	NEBRASKA

DEFENSE		
DL	**Hugh Green**	PITTSBURGH
DL	**Ross Browner**	NOTRE DAME
DL	**Lee Roy Selmon**	OKLAHOMA
DL	**Rich Glover**	NEBRASKA
LB	**Jack Ham**	PENN STATE
LB	**Randy Gradishar**	OHIO STATE
LB	**Jerry Robinson**	UCLA
DB	**Kenny Easley**	UCLA
DB	**Michael Haynes**	ARIZONA STATE
DB	**Tommy Casanova**	LSU
DB	**Jack Tatum**	OHIO STATE

> NICKNAMES <

Earl [The Tyler Rose] Campbell ∧
Ottis [O.J.] Anderson
Adolph [Bee-Beep] Bellizeare
Earnest Ray [Bubba] Bean
Charles [Boobie] Clark
Sam [Bam] Cunningham
[TD] Tony Dorsett
Donald Ray [Ike] Forte
Robert [Spider] Gaines
Archie [Butterball] Griffin
Michael [Luxury] Haynes
Don [The Dawgfather] James
Billy [White Shoes] Johnson
Gary [Big Hands] Johnson
Johnny [The Italian Stallion] Musso
Ozzie [The Wizard of Oz] Newsome
Joe [JoePa] Paterno
Walter [Sweetness] Payton
Randy [The Manster] White
Richard [Batman] Wood
Charles [Tree] Young

HEISMAN TROPHY WINNER

'70	**JIM PLUNKETT**	Stanford
'71	**PAT SULLIVAN**	Auburn
'72	**JOHNNY RODGERS**	Nebraska
'73	**JOHN CAPPELLETTI**	Penn State
'74	**ARCHIE GRIFFIN**	Ohio State
'75	**ARCHIE GRIFFIN**	Ohio State
'76	**TONY DORSETT**	Pitt
'77	**EARL CAMPBELL**	Texas
'78	**BILLY SIMS**	Oklahoma
'79	**CHARLES WHITE**	USC

RUSHING LEADER

		YARDS
ED MARINARO Cornell		158.3
ED MARINARO Cornell		209.0
PETE VAN VALKENBURG BYU		138.6
MARK KELLAR Northern Illinois		156.3
LOUIE GIAMMONA Utah State		153.4
RICKY BELL USC		170.5
TONY DORSETT Pittsburgh		177.1
EARL CAMPBELL Texas		158.5
BILLY SIMS Oklahoma		160.2
CHARLES WHITE USC		180.3

PASSING LEADER

		YARDS
SONNY SIXKILLER Washington		2,303
BRIAN SIPE San Diego State		2,532
DON STROCK, Virginia Tech		3,243
JESSE FREITAS San Diego State		2,993
STEVE BARTKOWSKI Cal		2,580
CRAIG PENROSE San Diego State		2,660
TOMMY KRAMER Rice		3,317
GUY BENJAMIN Stanford		2,521
STEVE DILS Stanford		2,943
TURK SCHONERT Stanford		163.0*

*EFFICIENCY RATING

>> THE DECADE'S DYNASTIES

Oklahoma >

The second golden age of Oklahoma football featured runners like Greg Pruitt, Joe Washington and 1978 Heisman winner Billy Sims as well as defenders such as the Selmon brothers. The Sooners won two national championships ('74 and '75 under Barry Switzer) and ranked in the Top 3 five other years, with a winning percentage (.887) that was the best for any program in a decade since the great Oklahoma teams of the '50s.

Alabama

Bear Bryant's Crimson Tide rode a rugged defense (led by linebacker Barry Krauss and DT Marty Lyons) to the decade's last two AP titles, adding to the 1973 UPI crown.

Nebraska

Wingback Johnny Rodgers (the 1972 Heisman winner) was the catalyst for coach Bob Devaney's '70 and '71 national champs, and the transition from Devaney to Tom Osborne (who took over in '73) was exceedingly smooth, as the Cornhuskers won at least nine games each year.

Notre Dame

A ferocious defensive end, Ross Browner, and a couple of not-so-ordinary Joes, Theismann and Montana, were the indispensable men at South Bend as two Irish coaches won national titles: Ara Parseghian in 1973 and Dan Devine in '77.

USC

The Trojans literally ran all over their opponents in the '70s: Sam Cunningham, Anthony Davis, Ricky Bell and Charles White ('79 Heisman) carried teams coached by John McKay and John Robinson to 21 total weeks at No. 1.

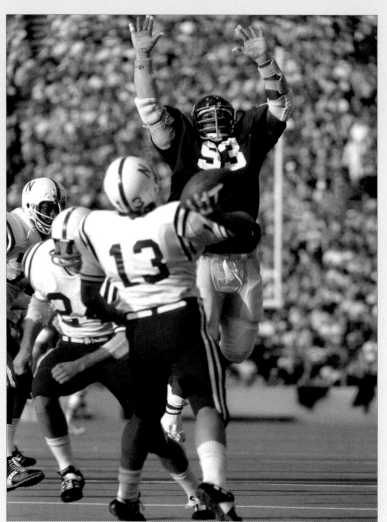

Lee Roy Selmon (93) and brothers Lucious and Dewey smothered Sooners foes.

> EPIC GAMES

<Nebraska *vs.* Oklahoma

November 25, 1971

This "game of the century" lived up to its hype: In a pulsating, back-and-forth affair in Norman, Jerry Tagge *(left)* and the No. 1 Cornhuskers nipped the No. 2 Sooners 35–31 on a fourth-quarter TD. The highlight-reel play was supplied by Nebraska wingback Johnny Rodgers, who darted and dashed to a first-quarter TD on a 72-yard punt return.

USC *vs.* Ohio State

January 1, 1975 · ROSE BOWL

Top pregame billing went to two premier rushers, Buckeyes Heisman Trophy winner Archie Griffin and the runner-up, the Trojans' Anthony Davis. But it was air power that proved decisive when, with 2:03 to go, USC QB Pat Haden's TD pass to Johnny McKay and subsequent conversion toss to Shelton Diggs gave the Trojans an 18–17 win.

Penn State *vs.* Alabama

January 1, 1979 · SUGAR BOWL

A classic fourth-quarter goal-line stand preserved a 14–7 Crimson Tide win and handed coach Bear Bryant his sixth and final national title. Alabama's Don Mc-Neal, David Hannah and Rich Wingo all made big stops, but the most memorable was linebacker Barry Krauss's stuffing of Nittany Lions back Mike Guman on fourth-and-goal from the one.

> CAMPUS CULTURE

YOU'VE GOT TO . . .

READ IT: *Deliverance*, James Dickey; *Love Story*, Erich Segal; *Watership Down*, Richard Adams; *Sophie's Choice*, William Styron; *Ball Four*, Jim Bouton; *Breakfast of Champions*, Kurt Vonnegut; *Dispatches*, Michael Herr; *All the President's Men*, Bob Woodward and Carl Bernstein; *Ragtime*, E. L. Doctorow; *Shogun*, James Clavell; *Roots*, Alex Haley; *The Complete Book of Running*, James Fixx

HEAR IT: Fleetwood Mac, Carole King, Joni Mitchell, Bee Gees, Earth, Wind & Fire, The Eagles, Led Zeppelin, Pink Floyd, Bob Marley, Elton John, The Who, KISS, Willie Nelson

SEE IT: *Rocky, Star Wars, Jaws, A Clockwork Orange, Superfly, The Godfather, Apocalypse Now, Saturday Night Fever, Halloween, Rocky Horror Picture Show, M*A*S*H, Monty Python, Saturday Night Live, Annie Hall, Charlie's Angels*

DISCUSS IT: Vietnam, Kent State, Watergate, Apollo 13, Camp David, Patty Hearst

DEAL WITH IT: The draft, Iran hostages, inflation, cocaine, Son of Sam, hijackings, Munich, Three Mile Island

HAVE IT: 8-track, pocket calculator, Pet Rock, muscle car, Pop Rocks, lava lamp

WEAR IT: Leisure suits, sideburns, afro, Earth Shoes, mood rings, bell-bottoms

DO IT: Disco, acupuncture, toga parties, line up for gas, march on Washington, streak

PLAY IT: Pong, ultimate frisbee, pinball

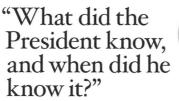

"What did the President know, and when did he know it?"

—Sen. Howard Baker (R., Tenn.) posed this question repeatedly during the Senate Watergate Committee hearings that began on June 25, 1973 and led to the resignation of Richard Nixon

Uninhibited or just ridiculous, streaking was the Me Decade's most naked ambition.

> SMARTEST GUY IN THE WORLD

STEPHEN HAWKING The inspirational British theoretical physicist formulated and popularized breakthrough theories of cosmology and black-hole dynamics despite physical debilitation from ALS (Lou Gehrig's disease).

> BY THE NUMBERS

472.4 Rushing yards per game for Oklahoma in 1971, a record.

31 Consecutive games in which Ohio State's Archie Griffin rushed for 100 yards or more.

60 Yardage exceeded on field goals (the first 65, then 64) by barefoot Texas A&M kicker Tony Franklin against Baylor on Oct. 16, 1976.

4 Teams that competed in the first Division 1-AA championship tournament, in 1978. Florida A&M defeated UMass in the final 35–28.

35.1 Yards per kickoff return for USC's Anthony Davis from 1972 to '74, an alltime career high.

209 Yards per game in 1971 for Cornell's Ed Marinaro, the nation's top rusher and the first player to average more than 200.

3 Consecutive years, from 1977 to '79, that a Stanford QB led the nation in passing. The Cardinals trio: Guy Benjamin, Steve Dils and Turk Schonert.

INNOVATOR

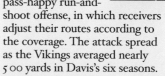

Mouse Davis As Portland State coach, Davis sped the spread of the pass-happy run-and-shoot offense, in which receivers adjust their routes according to the coverage. The attack spread as the Vikings averaged nearly 500 yards in Davis's six seasons.

1942 | PARTING THE Green Wave, Georgia's Frank Sinkwich (21) scampered for eight yards during a 40–0 romp over Tulane, kicking off a season in which the Bulldogs would win the Rose Bowl and Sinkwich the Heisman. | *Photograph by* AP

IT WASN'T A FLUKE.
IT WAS A FLUTIE

BY JOHN UNDERWOOD

Doug Flutie arched a last-second pass into the heavens that gave BC a miracle win. —*from* SI, DECEMBER 3, 1984

IT DOESN'T MATTER IF HE EVER PLAYS a down of pro football, although it would be nice. It doesn't matter if he ever quarterbacks another game for Boston College, although it will be necessary. It doesn't matter, because on one wildly wonderful play, Douglas Richard Flutie summed up a wildly wonderful college career last Friday in unsunny Miami. Never mind that he has two more games to play. They can only be anticlimactic.

Of course with Flutie you never know. Forty games into the most prolific passing career any college quarterback has ever had, you have to think in terms of clichés. With Flutie, says Gil Brandt of the Dallas Cowboys, life is a magic show, and "Doug Flutie never loses, he only runs out of time." But pick your own cliché. With Flutie, they all apply.

"It's not over until the last play"? This was Friday's final play: From the line of scrimmage, a Flutieball arched high into the Miami sky, covering 64 yards from toe to toe, to roommate Gerard Phelan—Flutie pushing off on his right toe and throwing into the gusting wind and rain, Phelan, in the end zone, falling directly behind and beneath the groping hands of two Miami defenders who were doing a stunning impersonation of an open door.

"It's the size of the fight in the man, not the size of the man in the fight"? At 5' 9¾"—if you don't give him the three-fourths, Flutie complains—little Dougie is not much bigger than the Heisman Trophy he will most certainly be awarded this week. Miami was the biggest team on his menu. And on a day better suited for ducks, the Eagles soared with Flutie, his passing alone accounting for 472 yards and three touchdowns, his running for nine yards and another TD. When the computers stopped humming, he had become the first 10,000-yard passer in major-college history. And when he went back outside an hour afterward, still in uniform so a friend could pose him in front of the Orange Bowl scoreboard, the evidence still glistened in the gloaming: Boston College 47, defending national champion Miami 45. Cast it in bronze and put it on the mantel.

There were more than a few touches of improbability in this victory. For in this game of breathtakingly proficient, precision passing, it was that most imprecise of passes that did the dirty deed. The Hail Mary. The Everybody Go Long. The play you launch on a wing and a prayer when all time is gone and all else has failed. In the BC playbook, it's called Flood Tip, and it works (rarely) the way it sounds.

With six seconds on the clock and Miami ahead 45–41, three BC receivers were deployed far to the right side, with Phelan as the middle man. At the snap they were to sprint downfield as fast and as far as they could, in hopes of arriving in the end zone together—flooding it—about the same time Flutie's pass got there. Such a play works "more often than you would think," says Flutie. "I'd say it's a 50-50."

It was Phelan that Flutie had found most often—10 times for 178 yards and a touchdown. Then, on the last play, when Phelan went by Hurricane defensive back Darrell Fullington (alas, a freshman), he was surprised that Fullington let him go. "He must have thought Doug couldn't throw it that far," Phelan said. Fullington and Reggie Sutton, another of the three Miami defenders in the area, backpedaled like outfielders and still were in good position right in front of the goal line as the fly ball came down.

Upfield, Miami had rushed only two men, and one of them, Jerome Brown, had squeezed through and chased Flutie out of the pocket and to his right. But that was exactly how Flutie wanted it. "The scrambling is important—it gives me the time I need on such a play," he said. (It's oh so matter of fact with Flutie, you understand.) "I knew I could throw it that far, even against the wind. I can throw 75 yards if I have to. Actually, I had to take a little off it to keep it in the end zone." (See?)

After he sidestepped Brown, Flutie circled back and around, and was at his 37-yard line when he came forward, planted his left foot and let fly. He said he "really did see Phelan break clear. He was the guy I wanted to get it to, but after I threw the ball, I didn't see anything much until the referee raised his arms. Then, I admit, I couldn't believe it, even when everybody started yelling and picking me up."

A fluke? Well, not really. A Flutie . . . .

FLUTIE FLUNG for 472 yards against the Hurricanes, but it was a Hail Mary heave to Phelan in darkness that landed the bantam Eagle among legends.

1982 | A MUSTANG in full gallop, Eric Dickerson (19) gained 4,450 yards and scored 48 touchdowns for SMU. | *Photograph by* RONALD C. MODRA

1987 | AS A Florida freshman, Emmitt Smith (22) torched Temple for 175 yards, one of his 23 100-yard rushing games as a Gator. | *Photograph by* BILL FRAKES

2005 | TROJAN TAILBACK Reggie Bush honored his Southern California area code while zipping for 8.7 yards per carry and a Heisman. | *Photograph by* MARK J. REBILAS

1963 | KANSAS COMET Gale Sayers could make defenders look like they were standing still, as he did on a 99-yard TD this day at Nebraska. | *Photograph by* RICH CLARKSON

A HELPING OF FAMILY VALUES

BY SALLY JENKINS

Miami's dynasty was sustained by former stars and their legacy of excellence—and arrogance. —*from* SI, AUGUST 31, 1992

PERHAPS THE SHEER LIGHTNESS of their surroundings makes the Miami Hurricanes run a step faster than everyone else. Everything seems easy in Ray-Ban land, down there in the world of the thong and the ankle tattoo. The Hurricanes seemed no different from other players when they were recruited by the more traditional football schools, but buried in their hearts must have been a little deviant individualism that led them to choose Miami, a school so seemingly, well, uncollegiate. It is only 67 years old. And the young men who play football for this school have the charm and arrogance of social-climbing bootleggers; they are the Jay Gatsbys of the NCAA. Yet they have manufactured tradition at an alarming pace, winning four national championships in nine years, including three in the last five and two in the last three.

Miami has gone 77–7 in the last seven seasons and finished in the top three in the country an unprecedented six straight times, accomplishments that demand comparison with the Notre Dame teams of the 1940s—the Irish won four national championships between 1943 and '49—and Oklahoma's teams of '53 through '57, which won 47 straight games and two national titles. Both of those dynasties were achieved under the direction of a single coach, Frank Leahy of the Irish and Bud Wilkinson of the Sooners. The Hurricanes, however, have won their four titles under three coaches—Howard Schnellenberger in '83, Jimmy Johnson in '87 and the incumbent, Dennis Erickson, in '89 and '91. Miami assistant coach Art Kehoe is the only member of the staff who has remained through all three administrations. He can honestly say, "I remember every loss."

The Hurricane program has become the maker of manners, the model for every coach and athletic director seeking to launch a winning tradition of his own. But is it possible to copy the Hurricanes? Probably not, for their success is the product of an elusive formula, a combination of many elements. Its essence is the players themselves, who, lacking any traditions of their own, decided to make some up as they went along.

The Miami alumni list of the last 10 years is an NFL Who's Who, and many of the entries can be found on the sideline at the Orange Bowl, where the Hurricanes have won 45 straight games. Bennie Blades, Melvin Bratton, Eddie Brown, Bernard Clark, Alonzo Highsmith, Michael Irvin, Jim Kelly, Brett Perriman and Daniel Stubbs are some of the current pros who can be spotted amid the orange jerseys. They chat. They clap. They cajole. They criticize. Frequently they threaten. They moan that the current Hurricanes aren't showy enough or throwy enough or talky enough or dancey enough. The alums even go so far as to call up current players at night and complain. It is the most effective form of alumni pressure in college football.

It begins with some hazing of the freshmen. It grows into a big-brother affair. It is not unusual to find three generations of Hurricane starters staying in touch with one another. Linebackers are especially close. Clark, who is now with the Dallas Cowboys, and Maurice Crum, a former All-America who also plays for the Cowboys, often take their undergraduate successors, Micheal Barrow and Darrin Smith, to breakfast at the New York, New York restaurant not far from campus.

Russell Maryland, the defensive lineman who anchored the '89 national-championship team and yet another Cowboy, also calls Barrow regularly. "It's handed down personally," says defensive end Rusty Medearis. "It's fed to you. From the first time you step on the field, that confidence is handed to you by the Hurricanes. You consume it, and you start playing like one."

During Smith's freshman year, in 1989, not long after he had moved into suite 36-A, his phone rang. When Smith picked it up, he heard an unfamiliar voice on the other end of the line. "Who's this?" the voice demanded. "What do you mean, Who's this?" Smith replied.

"I asked you first, who is *this*?" the voice said.

"This is Darrin Smith. Now who is this?"

"This is Michael Irvin," the voice said, "and you're in my room." . . .

> **Artifacts**

That's the Ticket!

Scores rise and fall, but one thing remains constant: The price of admission always leaves you with a keepsake of the game

MIAMI (OHIO) 25, NORTHWESTERN 14

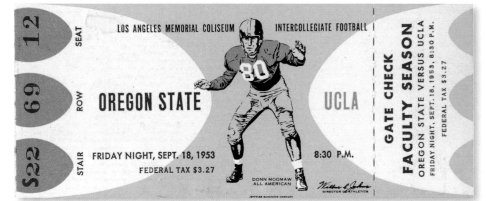

UCLA 41, OREGON STATE 0

OKLAHOMA 34, WASHINGTON STATE 14

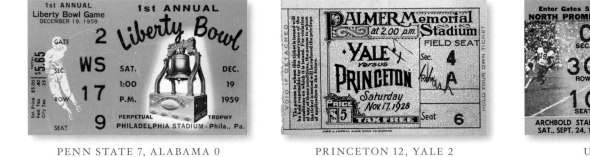

PENN STATE 7, ALABAMA 0

PRINCETON 12, YALE 2

UCLA 31, SYRACUSE 12

PHILADELPHIA
VETERANS STADIUM
PHILADELPHIA, PA.

SAT., DEC. 8, 1990

326 Sec.

12 Row

17 Seat

GAME TIME
T.B.A.

GATE B
LOWER STAND $28.50

ARMY

NAVY

100th
ANNIVERSARY
1890-1990

ARMY 30, NAVY 20

COTTON BOWL CLASSIC

ENTER GATE
2

ADMIT ONE
FRIDAY, JANUARY
1st, 1960 — 2:30 P.M.

Reserved Seat
PRICE $5.09
FED. TAX 41
TOTAL . . . $5.50

SEC. **103** ROW **21** SEAT **1**

DALLAS COTTON BOWL

SYRACUSE 23, TEXAS 14

SEAT **11**

ROW **4**

SEC. **121**

ENTER GATES 1-2-3-4 (Irving Avenue)
or GYM (North Field Stands)
ARCHBOLD STADIUM
SAT. NOV. 4, 1961 1:30 P.M. $3.50
ESTABLISHED PRICE $3.50

SYRACUSE
PITT

SYRACUSE 28, PITT 9

LEGION FIELD • BIRMINGHAM, ALABAMA

AUBURN vs. ALABAMA

LEGION FIELD

NO
PASS
OUT
CHECKS

SATURDAY **NOV. 28, 1981** 1:30 P.M.

NOT RESPONSIBLE FOR LOST, STOLEN OR MISPLACED TICKETS • VOID IF DETACHED

GATE **17**

SEC. **23**

ROW **48**

SEAT **15**

NORTH STAND
ALABAMA
NOV. 28, 1981

11 GAME

ALABAMA 28, AUBURN 17

Auspices
NEW ORLEANS
MID-WINTER
SPORTS ASS'N

NO
REFUND

25th
ANNIVERSARY
OF THE

SUGAR BOWL
Classic

SUGAR BOWL CLASSIC
New Orleans
1959

THURSDAY **JANUARY 1, 1959**
SEE CONDITIONS ON BACK

KICK-OFF 1:00 P.M.

EAST STAND
RAMP **2**
SEC. **2D**
ROW **15**
SEAT **8**

LSU 7, CLEMSON 0

1994 | THIS SAVAGE sack by Duke linebacker Willie McLaurin on Navy quarterback Jim Kubiak was a real head-turner. | *Photograph by* JOHN BIEVER

2006 | TYLER GRISHAM of Clemson was fortunate to lose nothing more than the ball when Georgia Tech safety Djay Jones collared him. | *Photograph by* DAVID BERGMAN

YOU LOVE WOODY OR HATE HIM

BY ROY TERRELL

When it came to Wayne Woodrow Hayes, there was no in-between.
—*from* SI, SEPTEMBER 24, 1962

OODY HAYES WILL BE 50 years old next Valentine's Day, if he makes it, and sometimes you wonder. Football is a happy game, even in the Big Ten. Chrysanthemum sales boom, old grads have a good excuse to get squiffed, hardly anyone goes to class, and if the halfback gets a black eye his girl will kiss it. Only Woody Hayes must suffer. To him, football is less a game than a 20th-century torture device, and on his own private rack, on a hundred Saturday afternoons in the vast stadiums of the Midwest, he has been subjected to agonies that would make your hair look like Harpo Marx's. While the avalanche of sound from 80,000 hysterics rolls down upon him, he stands alone, a short, powerful man with a barrel chest and a barrel stomach. It is cold, but he wears no coat. His hands are balled fists below his shirtsleeves, and perspiration streams from beneath the old gray baseball cap with the scarlet letter O, as in O-HI-O, that he has worn so long it now seems a part of his head. He prowls the sidelines like a bear in a pit, shouting in fury at the officials, snarling in frustration at his team, at his coaches, at himself. Deprive Woody Hayes of victory and he would die, just as surely as a man in space suddenly deprived of his oxygen supply; and so, until victory is assured, Woody dies. With each Ohio State mistake, with each fumble and penalty and interception, he dies. It would be a pitiful sight were it not for one thing: At the rate at which Ohio State makes mistakes, no one should have to worry about burying Hayes for at least another 132 years.

There was a time when the thought that Woody Hayes might go on forever would have set off only limited celebration in the Big Ten. Hayes has won four of the last eight conference championships, including last year's. The only losing season under Hayes came in 1959, when he tried to get fancy, a lapse that he now attributes to temporary insanity. Outside of that, Hayes has lost just nine games in the last eight years and, in one poll or another, Ohio State has three times been named the national champion. Success breeds its own antagonisms, and Woody Hayes would be the most surprised person in the world if the Big Ten should ever elect him Queen of the May.

But success alone can never explain the passion that Hayes has been known to arouse. You either love him or you hate him, and if you happen to be one of the few with no opinion you may just as well form one, since he probably has an opinion about you. He has an opinion about everything else.

If you choose to disapprove of Woody Hayes, there is a wide selection of reasons. He drives his players with a ferocity that would make a Marine Corps drill instructor look like Mary playing with her lamb. The football that he coaches—the crunching up-the-middle trap and off-tackle smash—is about as inspiring as a radish. It has furnished the sport with a now-tired phrase—three yards and a cloud of dust—and so far as you can discover in Columbus, Knute Rockne, Gus Dorais and the forward pass have not yet been invented.

Reporters assigned to cover the Ohio State dressing room decide to bury their grandmothers on days when it appears that the Buckeyes might not win. If Hayes is a bad loser—he has refused to shake hands with an opposing coach who beat him—he is also a bad winner, sometimes heaping scorn and humiliation upon a defeated opponent's head. He has a temper like a toothless cat. Most damning of all, he always says what he thinks. In fact Woody Hayes passes up more opportunities to keep his mouth shut in one year than most people do in a lifetime.

Through the years, Hayes has been in more scraps with opposing coaches, officials, reporters, university administrators, alumni and fans than he can count, if he bothers to count at all. He has not changed a whisker in all this time, but a strange thing has happened: The people around Woody Hayes are beginning to change. A former assistant, Rix Yard, once said, "Woody sticks to what he believes is right, even when it's wrong." In retrospect he has proved to be wrong so seldom (at least about football) that a slew of people who once opposed him are now on his side. He is suddenly in danger of becoming one of the most popular men in all Ohio, a fate that horrifies Hayes no end. "I'm not trying to win a popularity poll," he growls. "I'm trying to win football games." . . .

BUCKEYE BACKERS swore by him, foes swore *at* him, but no one could dispute the cantankerous Hayes's legacy: 13 Big Ten titles and three national crowns.

2000 | IT WASN'T a lack of electrifying action but dicey weather that forced cancellation of the game when Virginia Tech hosted Georgia Tech. | *Photograph by* ERIC BRADY

2007 | BRANDON DAY (34) and his Carroll College teammates were high muck-a-mucks after beating Sioux Falls for the NAIA title. | *Photograph by* JOHN RUSSELL

1965 | TEXAS TECH'S Tom Wilson (shown here in a win over Baylor) reared back and completed 61% of his passes for the 8–3 Red Raiders. | *Photograph by* WALTER IOOSS JR.

2006 | FLIPPING HIS trademark jump pass against LSU, Florida's Tim Tebow in '07 hopped to a Heisman, the first handed to a sophomore. | *Photograph by* JOHN BIEVER

MORE THAN GEORGIA'S ON HIS MIND

BY CURRY KIRKPATRICK

His roots are in the Deep South, but Herschel Walker sees the whole world as his stage. —*from SI, AUGUST 31, 1981*

YOU COULD SAY THAT WE BECOME what we are not so much in the sanctuary of the womb or the groves of academe but in that Elysian drive-in joint known as high school. This is especially true in the case of heroes who learn to be heroes in high school and stay that way. High school nerds can change and turn into real people, but high school heroes aren't permitted the luxury. So why all the hullabaloo over Herschel Junior Walker, 19 and never been hissed? Why such astonishment about his poise, intelligence, charm, graciousness, humility, charisma and his ability to put together more than two words at a time? Sir John Gielgud once said of Jean Seberg, who came out of little Marshalltown, Iowa, "She had learned to be a star before she became an actress." And so, now, Herschel Walker, the End Zone Stalker.

Walker, the All-America football player, says he runs track better than he plays football. Walker, the world-class sprinter, says he dances better than he sprints. Walker, the jump-splits hoofer, says he spends more time writing poetry than sashaying around the disco floor. But if there is one thing he knows more about than all of this, it is how to be a hero. Herschel Walker, out of little Wrightsville, Ga., learned that before he became anything else.

If all the Georgia Dawgs will please hunker down for a moment and cease woofing, we can put away Walker's historical debut against Tennessee and his historical NCAA freshman rushing record of 1,616 yards and his historical rookie-year third-place finish in the Heisman Trophy voting and his historical one-man-gang-despite-a-dislocated-shoulder Sugar Bowl routine against Notre Dame for the national championship and . . . woof, woof, woof. All right, all right.

On campus at Athens, Walker's behavior was nothing more than a finely tuned emulation of a value system taught by his parents, Willis and Christine. He was, and is, a child of the Old South, possessed of all that implies—gentility, courtesy, devotion to Sunday School, punctuality at supper, loyalty to home and hearth. He is sincerely a mama's boy, Christine Walker's boy through and through. When Walker arrived at the state university, a school that first gave an athletic scholarship to a black in 1968, the dynamic that shocked everyone was the fact that he was a black child of the Old South who hit the books, quoted from *Macbeth* and insisted he would graduate with a degree in criminology. And, besides, the guy could run the football a little bit.

Immediately Walker disarmed potential critics (read: the press) as easily as he evaded potential tacklers. Herschel, don't you get tired carrying the football so many times? "No, sir, the ball ain't heavy."

Running backs are forever being compared. Payton to Simpson to Sayers, Campbell to Brown to Motley. In reality such an exercise is futile because, like concert pianists, each RB has some distinct characteristic with which he delivers the goods. After one has rounded up clichés like *inner drive* and *concentration* and *competitiveness*, there is simply this about Walker—probably no runner has ever been so powerful and so fast concurrently.

Georgia's Vince Dooley, speaking in Early Colonial coachese, mentions Walker's feet. How "close together" and "close to the ground" they are. How he has "the nice base" and "the good plant and spurt." How he "slides" so well. Dooley says Walker's improvement graph in practices and games was a vast upward slope. "Herschel kept getting better and better. He just never leveled off."

The sine qua non for all running backs is their ability at that moment when the hole closes. Do they whirl, shift direction, lower the helmet? Spin off? Slow up? Power move? What Walker seems to do better than anyone before is to accelerate right then and there and whip into a gear unbeknownst to mere football players. Remember, we are talking about an Olympic gold medal aspirant who has run the 60-yard dash in 6.24 and a wind-aided 10.22 100 meters. We're talking quick. "Herschel won't impress you with his slick moves or feints," says Georgia running backs coach Mike Cavan. "But don't let him get even with you on the field or the points start clicking on the scoreboard." . . .

PART WHIPPET, all Bulldog, Walker scored his second TD to give Georgia a 17–10 win over Notre Dame in the Sugar Bowl—and the 1980 national title.

THE 1980s

> THE ALL-DECADE TEAM

OFFENSE		DEFENSE	
TE	**Keith Jackson** OKLAHOMA	DL	**Tony Casillas** OKLAHOMA
OL	**Jeff Bregel** USC	DL	**Tracy Rocker** AUBURN
OL	**Jimbo Covert** PITTSBURGH	DL	**Billy Ray Smith** ARKANSAS
OL	**Bill Fralic** PITTSBURGH	DL	**Reggie White** TENNESSEE
OL	**Tony Mandarich** MICHIGAN STATE	LB	**Chris Spielman** OHIO STATE
C	**Dave Rimington** NEBRASKA	LB	**Ricky Hunley** ARIZONA
WR	**Anthony Carter** MICHIGAN	LB	**Lawrence Taylor** NORTH CAROLINA
WR	**Jerry Rice** MISSISSIPPI VALLEY STATE	DB	**Deion Sanders** FLORIDA STATE
QB	**John Elway** STANFORD	DB	**Terry Kinard** CLEMSON
RB	**Marcus Allen** USC	DB	**Terry Hoage** GEORGIA
RB	**Herschel Walker** GEORGIA	DB	**Ronnie Lott** USC

> NICKNAMES <

Raghib [Rocket] Ismail ^
Willie [Flipper] Anderson
Norman [Boomer] Esiason
[Swervin'] Mervyn Fernandez
Craig [Ironhead] Heyward
Vincent [Bo] Jackson
A.J. [Jam] Jones
Lionel [Little Train] James
Karl [The Albino Rhino] Mecklenburg
Lyvonia [Stump] Mitchell
William [Bubba] Paris
William [The Refrigerator] Perry
[Neon] Deion Sanders
Tiaina [Junior] Seau
Willie [Satellite] Totten
Jessie [The Hammer] Tuggle
[Touchdown] Tommy Vardell
Reggie [The Minister of Defense] White
Elbert [Ickey] Woods
Harold E. [Butch] Woolfolk
Chris [Zorro] Zorich

	HEISMAN TROPHY WINNER	RUSHING LEADER		PASSING LEADER	
			YARDS PER GAME		EFFICIENCY
'80	**GEORGE ROGERS** South Carolina	**GEORGE ROGERS** South Carolina	**161.9**	**JIM McMAHON** BYU	**176.9**
'81	**MARCUS ALLEN** USC	**MARCUS ALLEN** USC	**212.9**	**JIM McMAHON** BYU	**155.0**
'82	**HERSCHEL WALKER** Georgia	**ERNEST ANDERSON** Oklahoma State	**170.6**	**TOM RAMSEY** UCLA	**153.5**
'83	**MIKE ROZIER** Nebraska	**MIKE ROZIER** Nebraska	**179.0**	**STEVE YOUNG** BYU	**168.5**
'84	**DOUG FLUTIE** Boston College	**KEITH BYARS** Ohio State	**150.5**	**DOUG FLUTIE** Boston College	**152.9**
'85	**BO JACKSON** Auburn	**LORENZO WHITE** Michigan State	**173.5**	**JIM HARBAUGH** Michigan	**163.7**
'86	**VINNY TESTAVERDE** Miami	**PAUL PALMER** Temple	**169.6**	**VINNY TESTAVERDE** Miami	**165.8**
'87	**TIM BROWN** Notre Dame	**ICKEY WOODS** UNLV	**150.7**	**DON McPHERSON** Syracuse	**164.3**
'88	**BARRY SANDERS** Oklahoma State	**BARRY SANDERS** Oklahoma State	**238.9**	**TIMM ROSENBACH** Wash. State	**162.0**
'89	**ANDRE WARE** Houston	**ANTHONY THOMPSON** Indiana	**163.0**	**TY DETMER** BYU	**175.6**

>> THE DECADE'S DYNASTIES

Miami >
Quarterback U emerged under Howard Schnellenberger, and the curriculum was refined by Jimmy Johnson, producing Jim Kelly, Bernie Kosar and 1986 Heisman winner Vinny Testaverde as well as three national titles. The Hurricanes faced top-ranked teams seven times and won all of those games.

Penn State
The Nittany Lions won national championships in 1982 and '86, although they were not ranked No. 1 until the final poll in either season. Joe Paterno trotted out one of his greatest linebackers, Shane Conlan, and a corps of superb runners including Curt Warner, D.J. Dozier and Blair Thomas.

Nebraska
Tom Osborne's Cornhuskers averaged a nation's-best 10.3 wins in the 1980s. Center Dave Rimington became the only back-to-back Outland Trophy winner ('81 and '82), and Mike Rozier ran for more than 2,000 yards to land the '83 Heisman.

Georgia
Few players define an era as Herschel Walker did for the early 1980s Bulldogs. Walker set 11 NCAA records during his three years in Athens, carrying his team to a perfect season and national title as a freshman in '80, and winning the Heisman in '82 when Georgia lost only to Penn State, in the Sugar Bowl.

Augustana
From 1983 to '86 the small Lutheran college in Rock Island, Ill., had a stranglehold on the Division III championship. Bob Reade's Vikings had six unbeaten regular seasons; in four of those he was National Small College Coach of the Year.

The Hurricanes won the arms race with sterling quarterbacks like Testaverde (14).

> EPIC GAMES

< Georgia *vs.* Florida
November 8, 1980

With 1:08 to go, pinned on his seven and trailing the Gators by a point, Bulldogs QB Buck Belue (*left*) hit wideout Lindsay Scott on a deep post pattern. Scott did the rest, outrunning the entire Florida secondary for the TD that propelled Georgia and freshman Herschel Walker (238 rushing yards) to a 26–21 win and the top of the polls.

Cal *vs.* Stanford
November 20, 1982

With four seconds left at Berkeley, the Cardinal had taken a one-point lead on a Mark Harmon field goal. The return of the ensuing kickoff went down in lore as the Play: five laterals, the last ending up with the Bears' Kevin Moen, who dashed into the end zone through the Stanford band, which had charged onto the field in premature celebration.

Boston College *vs.* Miami
November 23, 1984

The fourth TD of the day by Melvin Bratton had given Miami a four-point lead with 28 seconds to go, and the Eagles, 48 yards from pay dirt, needed a miracle. Prayer answered: Doug Flutie launched a Hail Mary into the Orange Bowl end zone that fell neatly into the hands of Gerard Phelan. The heave gave B.C. a 47–45 win and Flutie a Heisman.

> CAMPUS CULTURE

YOU'VE GOT TO...

READ IT: *Cosmos*, Carl Sagan; *The Bonfire of the Vanities*, Tom Wolfe; *Megatrends*, John Naisbitt; *Ironweed*, William Kennedy; *Love in the Times of Cholera*, Gabriel García Márquez; *Cultural Literacy*, E.D. Hirsch Jr.; *Pet Sematary*, Stephen King; *Patriot Games*, Tom Clancy

HEAR IT: Madonna, Michael Jackson, Prince, The Police, Bruce Springsteen, U2, R.E.M., Whitney Houston, Van Halen, Metallica, The Pretenders, Talking Heads

SEE IT: *Risky Business*, *Top Gun*, *Fatal Attraction*, *Scarface*, *This Is Spinal Tap*, *Ferris Bueller's Day Off*, *E.T.*, *Back to the Future*, *Die Hard*, *Lethal Weapon*, *Ghostbusters*, *Caddyshack*, *Dallas*, CNN, *The A-Team*, *Miami Vice*, *Cheers*

"Where's the beef?"

—Wendy's commercial catchphrase reprised by Democratic presidential candidate Walter F. Mondale, speaking to Sen. Gary Hart during a primary debate, March 11, 1984

DISCUSS IT: Tiananmen Square, collapse of the U.S.S.R, Sandra Day O'Connor, insider trading, African famine, Reaganomics, U.S. invasion of Grenada and Panama, Iran-Contra

DEAL WITH IT: The Exxon *Valdez*, Space Shuttle *Challenger*, smoking sections, Chernobyl, AIDS, crack, Yuppies, tainted Tylenol

HAVE IT: VCR, CD player, Atari, car phone, Windows, Walkman

WEAR IT: Power ties, Nike Air, Members Only jackets, Ray-Bans, turned-up polo shirt collars, leg-warmers, Jheri curls, ripped sweatshirts, shoulder pads, denim jackets

DO IT: Aerobics, break dancing, "Just say no," spring break

PLAY IT: Pac-Man, Rubik's Cube, Trivial Pursuit, hacky sack

Life was a beach during spring break, which became a de facto part of the school calendar.

> SMARTEST GUY IN THE WORLD

BILL GATES Along with childhood friend Paul Allen, Gates founded the software firm Microsoft, whose operating system for IBM computers would also make Gates (the copyright owner) the richest guy in the world.

> BY THE NUMBERS

238.9 Rushing yards per game by Oklahoma State's Barry Sanders in 1988, an alltime record.

771 Passing yards for Houston in a 95–21 defeat of SMU on Oct. 21, 1989.

3 Winless seasons for Northwestern in the 1980s. In '82 the Wildcats snapped their record NCAA losing streak of 34 games by beating Northern Illinois 31–6.

4,693 Receiving yards for Jerry Rice at Mississippi Valley State from 1981 to '84. Rice also had 301 receptions and 50 touchdown catches, all records that later were surpassed.

211 Combined points in 1983 by the Zendejas brothers, Arizona State's Luis (112) and Arizona's Max (99), who ranked first and second in the nation in scoring by a kicker.

49 Consecutive nonlosing seasons for Penn State, an NCAA record streak ended in 1988 when the Nittany Lions went 5–6.

INNOVATOR

LaVell Edwards In a run-oriented era, the BYU coach revitalized the spread formation, deploying as many as five receivers. His system produced QBs Jim McMahon, Robbie Bosco, Steve Young and Ty Detmer, and a host of disciples.

2007 | NORTH CAROLINA'S Deunta Williams went head over Tar Heels to break up a pass to Maryland's grounded Joey Haynos. | *Photograph by* STREETER LECKA

1998 | FLORIDA STATE'S Peter Warrick had a pleasant flight and a happy landing despite the late arrival of Miami's Leonard Myers. | *Photograph by* BOB ROSATO

> **Artifacts**

Nose Jobs

Long before masks became standard on helmets in the 1950s, players took elaborate measures to guard against facial blows

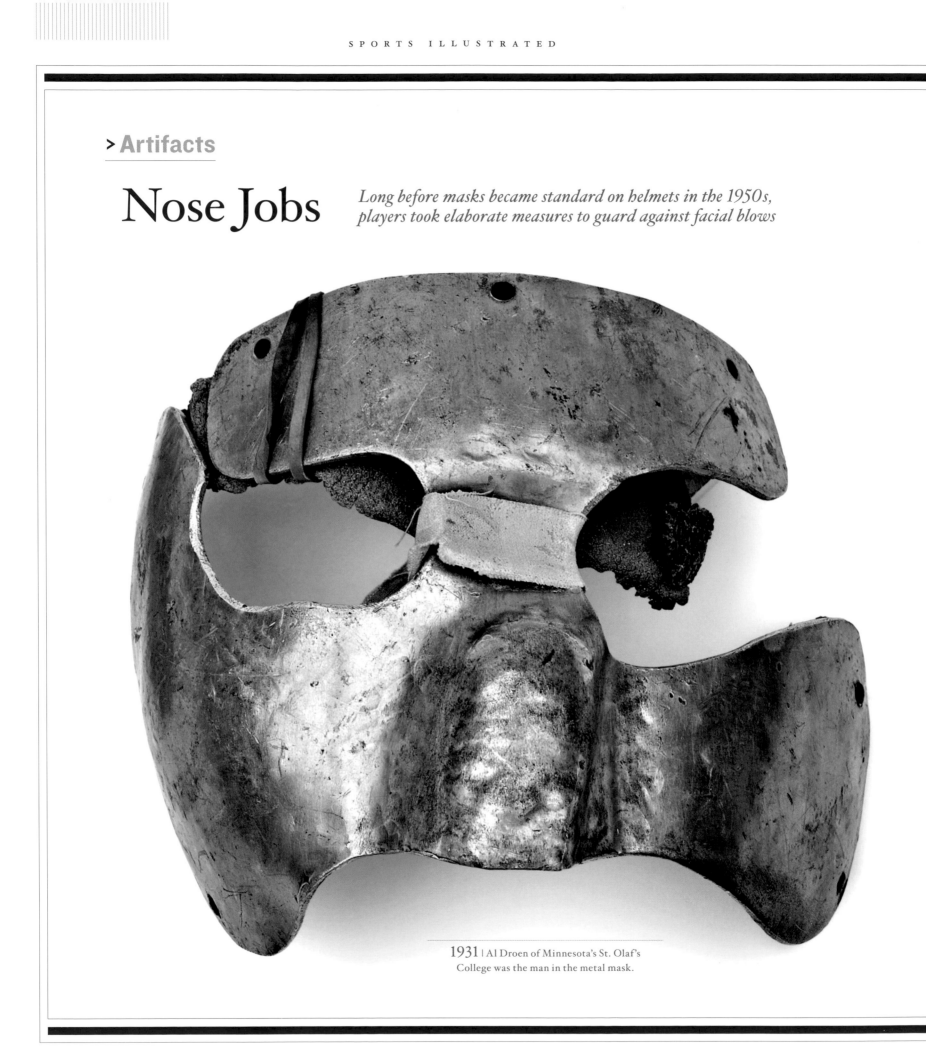

1931 | Al Droen of Minnesota's St. Olaf's College was the man in the metal mask.

1901 | Columbia's Hathaway Weeks
rigged a nose guard to his helmet.

1932 | Yale captain John Wilbur max-protected
the beak he broke against Princeton.

1890s | The metal Morrill's nose mask
was often personalized by its owner.

DAVID BERKWITZ (3); COLLEGE FOOTBALL HALL OF FAME; CORBIS (WILBUR)

THE HEART OF DIXIE

BY TIM LAYDEN

As a Tennessee quarterback, Peyton Manning made quite a name for himself, but in the SEC pantheon, Archie will forever be the Manning. —from SI, AUGUST 26, 1996

ARCHIE MANNING WENT TO Ole Miss in the fall of 1967 from the tiny Mississippi Delta town of Drew (pop. 2,143). By the end of his junior year he had restored the Rebels to a place among the nation's elite teams and had been hailed as perhaps the best quarterback in a national class that included Stanford's Jim Plunkett, Notre Dame's Joe Theismann, Santa Clara's Dan Pastorini and Ohio State's Rex Kern. Archie was also the object of a statewide adoration that hasn't abated 26 years later. "He was a legend, much larger than life," says author John Grisham, who grew up in Southaven, Miss.

Peyton Manning immersed himself in his father's college legacy after an Ole Miss fan sent his family audiotapes of the Rebels' epic 1969 upsets of Georgia and LSU. Peyton, then a junior in high school, popped the tapes into his stereo, lay across his bed and let history wash over him. He listened as his dad's offense, every member a Mississippian, was described by the play-by-play man: *"Manning brings 'em to the line. There's Mitchell from Columbus, Coker from Clarksdale . . . Manning sprints out right, throws . . . touchdown! Touchdown, Ole Miss!"* Peyton memorized the calls and embellished them: "Manning, the 6' 3" Drew redhead, brings 'em to the line . . . ."

He quizzed both his father and his mother, Olivia, the Ole Miss homecoming queen whom Archie married in 1971. They told him what college football was like, how magical Saturdays were, how they had double-dated with Archie's teammates and their steadies. Peyton embraced his father's past and formed a picture of his own future. He would be a quarterback, but not in the NFL. "Dad's college career was such a bright memory," says Cooper Manning, Peyton's older brother. "His pro career was . . . what? Guys in the Superdome with bags on their heads." So Peyton wouldn't aspire to be Marino or Phil Simms or Dan Fouts. "I never once heard him say, 'I want to be a pro football player,' " says his mother. "It was always, 'I want to play college foot-

ball.' " He would be a college quarterback. In the South. Just like Archie.

In his sophomore year at Isidore Newman, the private school in New Orleans that he attended from kindergarten, Peyton first questioned his father about studying game film. This was logical, because his father played quarterback in the NFL for 14 years. Archie didn't push his son to study film then; the quality of tapes from high school games wasn't very good anyway. But two years later, when Peyton expressed an interest in perusing some NFL game films, Archie told him, "If you're going to watch film, do it the right way." By that he meant, Don't watch the ball, watch the defense; fans watch the ball.

With this tiny piece of advice Archie helped create a monster who watches more videotape than Bob Saget. Last September, in the six days leading to Tennessee's drubbing by Florida, Manning watched more than 20 hours of tape on his own. In February his apartment mates moved Manning's VCR to the living room. "We figured maybe we could bring dates over and watch movies," says Vols senior linebacker Greg Johnson, one of Manning's best friends on the team. "That lasted maybe a month." The VCR was moved back to Manning's room.

Manning's apartment mates call him Caveman and his bedroom the Cave. On Saturday nights after home games he often returns to his apartment to watch a tape of the game. "I'm guessing most college players are out celebrating on Saturday night," says Ashley Thompson, the 21-year-old University of Virginia senior whom Manning has dated since they met in the fall of 1994. ("Even Peyton's love life is set up pretty well," says his father. "He's crazy about Ashley, but he just doesn't have time for a girlfriend on campus.")

And if he is not quite the folk hero in the South that his father was—who could be?—Peyton is still a celebrity. But he is not seeking such stardom; he is chasing an entire life— one that he has sought to re-create since he first listened to those Ole Miss tapes in high school. He can recite his father's Rebel lineups still: "Jernigan from Jackson, McClure from Hattiesburg . . . ." When he finishes, he gives a lopsided smile, the way he does when something strikes him as sweet or funny. "I would love to have played in the '60s," he says. "Now *that* would have been fun." . . .

REBEL YELLS gave rise to the legend of Archie (in '69) at Ole Miss, lending him a mystique that even his worthy SEC offspring, Peyton and Eli, wouldn't match.

1992 | EVEN STANDING on his head, USC's Jason Sehorn made an interception under San Diego State's airborne Ray Peterson. | *Photograph by* RICHARD MACKSON

1994 | CORNHUSKERS FANS were doing backflips after a two-yard touchdown by Nebraska's Damon Benning (21) in a 49–21 win over UCLA. | *Photograph by* JOHN BIEVER

1941 | A BROKEN JAW shielded by a jury-rigged harness, Georgia's Frank Sinkwich put his best face forward in a victory at Columbia. | *Photograph by* ACME/CORBIS

2002 | A FORTRESS-LIKE face mask couldn't guard against mud or disappointment for Nicholas Nelthorpe when Holy Cross fell to Lehigh. | *Photograph by* PAUL KAPTEYN

THE NIGHT IS YOUNG'S

BY AUSTIN MURPHY

In perhaps the most stunning bowl performance ever, Texas quarterback Vince Young carried the Longhorns to the title.
—*from* SI, JANUARY 9, 2006

UNDER A BLIZZARD OF SILVER confetti, in what had become a mosh pit on the field at the Rose Bowl on Wednesday night, arguably the greatest athlete in the world seemed overwhelmed by the moment. "Unbelievable," Lance Armstrong, clad in a burnt-orange T-shirt repeated, over and over. "This is just unbelievable." Or was it? When a player is as transcendent, as ridiculously dominant as Texas quarterback Vince Young was against the USC Trojans, and when a Pete Carroll–coached defense is made to look like so many cardinal-and-gold pylons, the Longhorns' breathtaking 41–38 victory is easily believable. As Longhorns right tackle Justin Blalock said while celebrating on the field, not far from where Armstrong posed for pictures with a gaggle of Texas cheerleaders, "We kept our poise, put the ball in Vince's hands and let the man do what he does."

All Young did was outplay a pair of Heisman Trophy winners, amassing 467 yards of total offense. He completed 30 of 40 passes for 267 yards and ran 19 times for 200 yards and three touchdowns. His last carry, on fourth-and-five from the USC eight-yard line with 19 seconds to play, went for the touchdown that clinched the Longhorns' first national title in 35 years. It also left a loquacious man at a temporary loss for words. "I've been planning this speech for 33 years," coach Mack Brown told his players in the winners' locker room, "but right now I don't really know what to say."

Upon arriving in Austin in the summer of '02, Young was still a raw talent who had much to learn from Brown and was, in fact, red-shirted. But make no mistake, on Wednesday night Texas won its fourth national title because Brown's relationship with his star quarterback had become a two-way street: The teacher learned a thing or two from his student as well.

Five straight losses to Oklahoma from 2000 through '04, all in the Cotton Bowl in Dallas, overshadowed otherwise excellent Texas seasons and threatened to define Brown's career. Each of those defeats was marked by a discernible tightness passed from the coaches to the players, a fear of failure. Young's career as a Longhorn can be viewed in part as a battle to overcome this constrictive atmosphere—a battle he officially won last season, when Brown and offensive coordinator Greg Davis gave up trying to fix his three-quarter throwing motion and attempting to transform him into a sprint-out, bootleg quarterback. They gave Young more latitude away from the field as well, signing off on his request to liven up the locker room and practices with song and dance—and we're not talking Lawrence Welk. Young even got Brown, 54, to loosen up by exposing him to the world of hip-hop, earning the coach a nickname from the team's beat writers: Snoop Mack.

After the game Carroll said that he had never coached against a player as totally commanding as Young had been. "He probably made us miss a dozen tackles tonight," Carroll said. In truth that estimate seemed low by at least a dozen.

Save for a spectacular 26-yard, fourth-quarter touchdown run on which he dived into the end zone, Reggie Bush, USC's Heisman Trophy–winning halfback, took a backseat to LenDale White, whose thunderous inside runs (he rushed for 124 yards and three touchdowns), coupled with the precision passing of Matt Leinart (the '04 Heisman winner), got the Trojans back into the game. In the second half USC ran off 28 points and never punted. But on fourth-and-one at the Texas 45 with 2:13 left, Carroll opted to go for it. Gain one yard, win the game. "We just blitzed everyone," said Texas safety Michael Huff, who helped stuff White inches shy. Young would have one final chance.

After he moved the Longhorns 48 yards in nine plays, the 2005 college football season came down to a single snap. Out of the shotgun Young looked to pass. "I went all the way through my progression," he recalled later, "but there was nobody open." Linebacker Collin Ashton and corner Josh Pinkard blitzed, but they were picked up by the Texas front, which didn't allow a sack all night. "The defensive lineman was giving me the edge"—that was Frostee Rucker, who dived vainly at Young's ankles—"so I took it down."

Young took the ball down, then he took the Trojans down.

Leaving the press conference as a losing coach for the first time since Sept. 27, 2003, Carroll smiled and asked, "What are you gonna do?" Disappearing down the corridor, he flashed USC's familiar two-fingered salute. It is intended to symbolize V, for victory. On this night, the V stood for something else. . . .

YOUNG'S STRETCH past the pylon and USC safety Scott Ware in the third quarter brought Texas from behind, but was a mere warmup for the finale.

2000 | RUNNING THROUGH the raindrops but not the Eagles, Ben Drinkwalter of the Montana Grizzlies was halted by David Young and Jamar Jones during the Division 1-AA title game, won by Georgia Southern 27–25. | *Photograph by* RYAN McKEE

1904 | After they were officially approved in the 1903 rules, wooden cleats soon caught on.

1939 | Duke back George McAfee went for speed with low-cuts and traction with metal cleats.

1950 | The jet age yielded the plastic cleat, lighter if perhaps less penetrating than metal.

1930s | Rubber cleats and hightops were standard issue on early grass fields.

> **Artifacts**

Firm Footing

Taking hold by the early 20th century, the cleat was reinvented repeatedly as field conditions changed

1996 | The new-age Nikes of Randy Moss were ideal for swift cuts on artificial turf.

DAVID BERGMAN (5), COLLEGE FOOTBALL HALL OF FAME

ST. MARY'S GLAMOROUS GALLOPING GAELS

BY FRANK GRAHAM JR.

Slip Madigan was as much a showman as football coach, and he brought fame to an obscure college by staging a great act with a colorful team. —*from* SI, NOVEMBER 13, 1967

I T IS 1936 AND A STRING OF 18 PULLMAN and baggage cars is moving slowly eastward out of California's Moraga Valley. Were we to peep into one of the Pullmans, we might feel for a moment that we were snooping on a musical film stage with dances by Busby Berkeley. True, Dick Powell cannot actually be seen singing to a coed, but his presence is somehow felt. If an assistant director should come by and if we were to ask him, he would tell us that this is no movie, it is simply the football team of tiny St. Mary's College setting forth once again to lay siege to another famed citadel of football and Catholicism. St. Mary's players make up only a fraction of the expeditionary force. They are accompanied by more than 200 singing, swinging businessmen, shopkeepers, secretaries and other camp followers, described as loyal fans of St. Mary's and its high-pressure coach, Edward Patrick (Slip) Madigan.

In addition to its sleeping, dining and reveling facilities, the St. Mary's Special contained a "gym car" equipped with rubdown tables, exercise mats, bucking machines for the linemen's use and a battery of showers. At the other side of the continent, where St. Mary's was scheduled to play Fordham in the Polo Grounds, New Yorkers followed the party's four-day journey. Wherever the train stopped, as it did in Chicago to give the players a chance to work out on the turf at Soldier Field, bulletins were flashed to New York. This "hard news" supplemented the press releases dispatched earlier by Madigan and his imaginative press agents.

Though St. Mary's College antedated Madigan, its existence had been a well-kept secret until Slip arrived. Fewer than 100 students were enrolled there in 1920 when its football team earned a small measure of notice by losing to California 127–0. The following autumn the Christian Brothers who ran the school hired Madigan to help spare it such unwanted publicity. Slip, who had played center under Knute Rockne at Notre Dame, was a large, cocky Irishman with a booming voice and a louder wardrobe. He set to work assembling husky young men to preserve the school's honor and a sufficient number of uniforms to clothe them. Within a year his team went down with all flags flying before powerful California 21–0.

A year or two later, the frequency with which it was upsetting its better-known rivals gained St. Mary's the reputation of a "giant killer." By that time Madigan had dubbed his team "the Galloping Gaels." As increasing gate receipts enriched St. Mary's treasury, the school moved out of its dingy building in Oakland and found a bright new campus in the Moraga Valley. At the same time Madigan began to shun the dark plumage worn by conventional teams of that era in favor of the wildest colors in the rainbow. He experimented with tearaway jerseys as well as the T formation. Rival coaches also accused him of concocting the "forward fumble" to pick up vital yardage.

In 1930 Madigan arranged to play Fordham annually in New York. St. Mary's president at first objected to the plan, fearing that the players would lose too much time from their classes. But Madigan argued persuasively that the many educational opportunities such a trip presented far outweighed the loss of class time. And by 1936 the St. Mary's–Fordham game had become a football attraction in New York second only to the Army–Notre Dame game. There were 50,000 people in the Polo Grounds that year when the St. Mary's players, glittering in their red silk jerseys with white epaulets and their shiny green pants, rushed onto the field. Strolling proudly after them, no less resplendent, was Coach Madigan in a natty light suit, pink shirt and orange cravat.

By the end of the first period, Slip looked as rumpled as his players. Storming up and down the sidelines, ranting at the officials, pulling his hat down over his ears, he worked himself into a lather. At halftime the Fordham band formed a giant tolling bell on the field and played *The Bells of St. Mary's.* The hungover camp followers, sitting together in the upper stands, cheered wildly and rained confetti down on the sidelines.

Shortly after St. Mary's lost the game, 7–6, the special train pulled out of New York. In addition to memories of another lively visit to the Big Town, Madigan carried with him a check for $38,824.15—St. Mary's share of the gate receipts. . . .

THE MADCAP Madigan (with fullback Thurman Black in 1922) put St. Mary's on the gridiron map with sharp coaching and all-American publicity.

1991 | A LOSS to Cal was no surprise but seemed upsetting enough to make UCLA's Michael Moore hide his head in the sand. | *Photograph by* PETER READ MILLER

1995 | JAMAL POLLOCK (33) of Williams kept it relatively clean as he planted his foot and the head of Amherst's Peter McConville. | *Photograph by* CHUCK SOLOMON

> THE ALL-DECADE TEAM

OFFENSE

TE	Marco Battaglia	RUTGERS
OL	Orlando Pace	OHIO STATE
OL	Jonathan Ogden	UCLA
OL	Jason Odom	FLORIDA
OL	Will Shields	NEBRASKA
C	Jay Leeuwenburg	COLORADO
WR	Raghib Ismail	NOTRE DAME
WR	Desmond Howard	MICHIGAN
QB	Peyton Manning	TENNESSEE
RB	Ricky Williams	TEXAS
RB	Marshall Faulk	SAN DIEGO STATE

DEFENSE

DL	Courtney Brown	PENN STATE
DL	Warren Sapp	MIAMI
DL	Steve Emtman	WASHINGTON
DL	Grant Wistrom	NEBRASKA
LB	Marvin Jones	FLORIDA STATE
LB	Ray Lewis	MIAMI
LB	LaVar Arrington	PENN STATE
DB	Terrell Buckley	FLORIDA STATE
DB	Champ Bailey	GEORGIA
DB	Dre' Bly	NORTH CAROLINA
DB	Charles Woodson	MICHIGAN

> NICKNAMES <

Jake [The Snake] Plummer ^
Flozell [The Hotel] Adams
Mike [A-Train] Alstott
Roland [Champ] Bailey
Atiim [Tiki] Barber
Martin [Automatica] Gramatica
Dimetry [Vonnie] Holliday
Qadry [The Missile] Ismail
Edgerrin [The Edge] James
Sebastian [Sea Bass] Janikowski
Marvin [Shade Tree] Jones
Andy [The Big Kat] Katzenmoyer
Tajuan [Ty] Law
Anthony [Booger] McFarland
Steve [Air] McNair
David [The Deuce] Palmer
Jeff [Jurassic] Paulk
Pat [Hit Man] Tillman
Dan [Big Daddy] Wilkinson
Floyd [Pork Chop] Womack
[Famous] Amos Zereoue

HEISMAN TROPHY WINNER

'90	TY DETMER BYU
'91	DESMOND HOWARD Michigan
'92	GINO TORRETTA Miami
'93	CHARLIE WARD Florida State
'94	RASHAAN SALAAM Colorado
'95	EDDIE GEORGE Ohio State
'96	DANNY WUERFFEL Florida
'97	CHARLES WOODSON Michigan
'98	RICKY WILLIAMS Texas
'99	RON DAYNE Wisconsin

RUSHING LEADER

	YARDS PER GAME
GERALD HUDSON Oklahoma State	149.3
MARSHALL FAULK San Diego State	158.8
MARSHALL FAULK San Diego State	163.0
LeSHON JOHNSON Northern Illinois	179.6
RASHAAN SALAAM Colorado	186.8
TROY DAVIS Iowa State	182.7
TROY DAVIS Iowa State	198.6
RICKY WILLIAMS Texas	172.1
RICKY WILLIAMS Texas	193.1
LaDAINIAN TOMLINSON TCU	168.2

PASSING LEADER

	EFFICIENCY
SHAWN MOORE Virginia	160.7
ELVIS GRBAC Michigan	169.0
ELVIS GRBAC Michigan	154.2
TRENT DILFER Fresno State	173.1
KERRY COLLINS Penn State	172.9
DANNY WUERFFEL Florida	178.4
STEVE SARKISIAN BYU	173.6
CADE McNOWN UCLA	168.6
SHAUN KING Tulane	183.3
MICHAEL VICK Virginia Tech	180.4

>> THE DECADE'S DYNASTIES

Nebraska >
The Cornhuskers dominated the mid-1990s, winning three national titles in four seasons under Tom Osborne, who unleashed his Black Shirts defense and a rushing attack spearheaded by Tommie Frazier, Ahman Green and Lawrence Phillips. Nebraska had an .868 winning percentage during the decade.

Florida State
By continually reloading on offense with the likes of RB Warrick Dunn and Heisman-winning QBs Charlie Ward (1993) and Chris Weinke (2000), and on defense with such studs as LBs Derrick Brooks and Peter Boulware, Bobby Bowden's crew lost only 13 of its 123 games and topped the AP poll 56 times, including a wire-to-wire run at No. 1 in 1999.

Miami
"The U" used power to intimidate foes and speed to bury them in the early 1990s. With Russell Maryland, Warren Sapp, Micheal Barrow and Ray Lewis on defense and '92 Heisman-winning quarterback Gino Torretta guiding the offense, the Hurricanes appeared in six straight New Year's Day bowl games and won the '91 national title under Dennis Erickson.

Tennessee
Phillip Fulmer steered the Vols to five double-digit win seasons, two SEC titles and the national championship in 1998, the year after the graduation of All-America QB Peyton Manning.

Youngstown State
Jim Tressel's Penguins won four Division I-AA titles before falling in 1999 to Georgia Southern in Youngstown's sixth trip to the championship game in the decade.

Winning back-to-back titles, Frazier (15) and Nebraska were a Big Red machine.

> EPIC GAMES

<Colorado *vs.* Michigan
September 24, 1994

The Buffaloes trailed by 12 with just over two minutes to go at the Big House in Ann Arbor when QB Kordell Stewart orchestrated two TD drives. The second culminated in a 73-yard pass tipped into the arms of receiver Michael Westbrook with no time left to give Colorado a 27–26 win on what will forever be known in Boulder as the Catch.

Florida State *vs.* Notre Dame
November 13, 1993

The No. 2 Irish jumped to a 24–7 lead over the No. 1 Seminoles in South Bend and held their top runner, Warrick Dunn, to 18 yards, yet had to stave off a comeback by QB Charlie Ward for a 31–24 triumph. The eventual Heisman winner's last-gasp pass to tie was knocked down at the goal line by cornerback Shawn Wooden.

Alabama *vs.* Miami
January 1, 1993 • SUGAR BOWL

Crimson Tide safety George Teague helped subdue the Hurricanes 34–13. The senior's 31-yard third-quarter interception of a Gino Torretta pass put Alabama up 27–6. In the fourth quarter with Miami's Lamar Thomas on his way to a touchdown, Teague ran him down and ripped the ball away, clinching Alabama's first national title in 14 years.

> CAMPUS CULTURE

YOU'VE GOT TO . . .

READ IT *Into Thin Air,* Jon Krakauer; *The Firm,* John Grisham; *Den of Thieves,* James B. Stewart; *Angela's Ashes,* Frank McCourt; *Men Are from Mars, Women Are from Venus,* John Gray; *Tuesdays with Morrie,* Mitch Albom; *The Perfect Storm,* Sebastian Junger

HEAR IT: Nirvana, Phish, Guns N' Roses, Green Day, Jay-Z, Dr. Dre, Pearl Jam, Dave Matthews Band, Radiohead, Red Hot Chili Peppers, Jane's Addiction, Billy Ray Cyrus, Puff Daddy, Notorious B.I.G., Tupac Shakur, Spice Girls, Dixie Chicks, Boyz II Men

SEE IT: *Titanic, Wayne's World, Goodfellas, Pulp Fiction, Saving Private Ryan, Schindler's List, The Simpsons, Friends, The Real World, Ally McBeal, Seinfeld, Law & Order, The West Wing, Melrose Place, South Park*

DISCUSS IT: Nelson Mandela, Hubble telescope, Dolly the cloned sheep, the World Wide Web, Michael Jordan, Rush Limbaugh

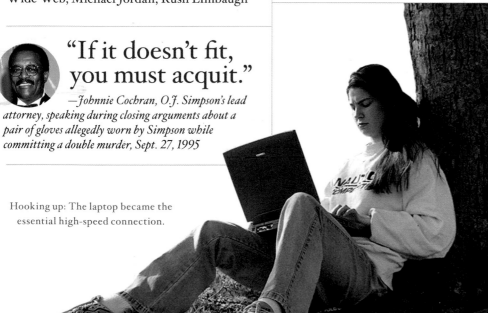

"If it doesn't fit, you must acquit."

—Johnnie Cochran, O.J. Simpson's lead attorney, speaking during closing arguments about a pair of gloves allegedly worn by Simpson while committing a double murder, Sept. 27, 1995

Hooking up: The laptop became the essential high-speed connection.

DEAL WITH IT: Rodney King, the O.J. trial, Monica Lewinsky, Columbine, Oklahoma City, 1994 baseball strike

HAVE IT: Piercings, digital camera, laptop, high-speed Internet, DVD, cellphone

WEAR IT: Torn jeans, flannel shirts, cargo pants, Spandex, baseball caps, boxers, bare midriffs, tooth grills

DO IT: Napster, the Macarena, get green, Rock the Vote, Rollerblading, snowboarding

PLAY IT: Golf, *Madden Football, Doom,* beer pong

> SMARTEST GUY IN THE WORLD

TIM BERNERS-LEE, a British born computer scientist who in 1990 formed the World Wide Web, dramatically broadening access to a network established a year earlier as a means for researchers to share up-to-date information.

> BY THE NUMBERS

8 Rushing touchdowns by Howard Griffith of Illinois in a 56–21 win over Southern Illinois on Sept. 22, 1990—a single-game record, as are Griffith's 48 points.

12.1 Points per game from 1991 to '93 by San Diego State's Marshall Faulk, tops in the modern era.

78 Career touchdowns by Travis Prentice of Miami (Ohio), breaking the record of 75 set a year earlier, in 1998, by Texas' Ricky Williams.

1 Number of Heisman Trophy winners coached by a previous Heisman winner. In 1996 Florida quarterback Danny Wuerffel played for Steve Spurrier, the '66 honoree.

0 Sacks allowed by Ohio State tackle Orlando Pace in 1995 and '96, his last two college seasons.

58 Consecutive games won at the Orange Bowl by Miami before a 38–20 loss to Washington on Oct. 3, 1994.

9 Wins in 1999 for Hawaii— nine more than in '98 and the largest single-season improvement in Division I-A history.

INNOVATOR

Roy Kramer The former SEC commissioner was the driving force behind the creation in 1998 of the Bowl Championship Series that guarantees a meeting between the nation's top two teams in a bowl that rotates each season.

GROUND BREAKERS

BY ALEXANDER WOLFF

Long after Jackie Robinson smashed baseball's color barrier, Southern college football was still a white man's game.

—*from* SI, NOVEMBER 7, 2005

FOR MOST WHITE SOUTHERNERS in the early Sixties, it was one thing to integrate their classrooms and quite another to desegregate their football teams. In the Southeastern, Atlantic Coast and Southwest conferences, and at such major independents as Houston, Florida State and Georgia Tech, to do so was to mess with the sacraments.

It took Jerry LeVias, the first black scholarship player in the Southwest Conference, much of his career at Southern Methodist to change that by earning the respect of his teammates and changing the perception of fans. One player spit in his face during a practice in 1965, his freshman season. Students scrambled to avoid having to sit next to him in class, and student trainers refused to tape his ankles. LeVias quickly learned to linger on the practice field so he wouldn't have to watch the shower stalls empty as soon as he entered them. As a sophomore LeVias became an instant, off-the-charts star, and he was the Mustang most likely to be acclaimed by the media after a victory. "And then," he says, "I was the skunk in the middle of the room."

LeVias had had no idea what awaited him when he arrived from segregated Beaumont, Texas, with a copy of the New Testament in his pocket. SMU coach Hayden Fry had signed him largely because of the verdict of Jerry's devout grandmother, who, after meeting Fry, told her grandson, "There's something godly about that man." Says LeVias, "We never did talk about breaking barriers. It says something about fate and faith—that's how I went to SMU." At one point in LeVias's recruitment his father, Charlie, asked where Southern Methodist was. Told it was in Dallas, he said, "They shot the president there. What they gonna do to my boy?"

Essentially anything they wanted to. At 5' 8" and 160 pounds, deployed on the flanks and on returns, LeVias was easy to target. LeVias met often with Fry to unburden himself of the abuse he took, always late at night because his coach didn't want other players to think LeVias was being coddled. Over and over Fry incanted a West Texasism: "If you don't want 'em to get your goat, don't let 'em know where it's hid." When the Mustangs went on the road, fans at Texas held up ropes tied into nooses, and the Texas A&M corps of cadets let black cats onto the field. As SMU, long a conference doormat, kept winning through the fall of 1966, the hate mail grew nastier. After LeVias emerged beaten up from a victory over Baylor that pushed the Mustangs' record to 7–2, Fry finally laid out for the press what his star had been going through and issued a plea that it stop. Other conference coaches indignantly denied any problem.

Several weeks later, before the season finale at TCU, someone phoned the SMU administration and vowed to shoot "that dirty nigger LeVias." Only just before kickoff did Fry tell his star of the threat. LeVias spent the game crouched down in the middle of huddles. And every Mustangs play began with a quick count. "I ran quicker to the bench than I did for a touchdown," LeVias says of his 68-yard pass play in that 21–0 victory, which sent SMU to its first Cotton Bowl since Doak Walker's days.

No racial trailblazer was as jaw-slackeningly good. LeVias touched the ball only 66 times all season, catching just 18 passes, yet in seven of SMU's eight victories he either scored or set up the Mustangs' winning points. The press gave Fry heat for not using him more, although LeVias never held it against his coach. "He was protecting me," LeVias says today.

LeVias had a knack for making opponents pay—as he puts it, "Turn the other cheek, then show them both cheeks" as you cross the goal line. During LeVias's senior season, with the Mustangs tied in the fourth quarter at TCU, a Horned Frogs linebacker tackling him said, "Go home, nigger!" and spit in his face. LeVias stalked off the field, flung his helmet against a wall and declared, "I quit!" He sat at the end of the bench and broke down in tears. Fry pleaded with him while the SMU defense held, and soon the Frogs were lining up to punt. As Fry scrambled to find a return man, LeVias bolted past him and onto the field, turning to say, "Coach, I'm gonna run this one back all the way."

"It was kind of like the Babe Ruth story," says Fry, who had picked up LeVias's headgear. "I handed him his helmet and said, 'Jerry, you might be needing this.'" Breaking down the film, Mustangs coaches would count 11 eluded tacklers, several of whom had two shots at him, and a couple of reverses of field during LeVias's 89-yard return for the decisive touchdown. . . .

THE FIRST prominent black player in the SWC, the 5' 8" LeVias confronted not only hostile tacklers but also bigotry—even in his own locker room.

2006 | IT WAS hats off to Cal's Marshawn Lynch, who ran for 152 yards and scored twice in the Bears' 21–3 mauling of Washington State. | *Photograph by* JOHN W. MCDONOUGH

2006 | NO HELMET? No matter to Pitt's Rashaad Duncan, who went head-on anyway into South Florida quarterback Pat Julmiste. | *Photograph by* AL MESSERSCHMIDT

DAVID BERKWITZ; COLLEGE FOOTBALL HALL OF FAME; COURTESY OF JACK L. KAAUA JR. (SKETCH)

A Cagey Contraption

In 1934 Hawaii guard Jack Kaaua suffered a career-threatening poke in the eye. To prevent further damage, he welded together a steel cage and mounted it on his helmet. Kaaua later wore his invention at Nebraska, Ohio State and Texas Tech, two decades before the cage would dominate the line of scrimmage.

IN HIS original plans, Kaaua included gogglelike glass lenses as the last line of defense against inadvertent or intentional eye gougers.

1966 | STOIC DURING a loss to Notre Dame, Purdue quarterback Bob Griese got the last laugh as the star of the Boilermakers' Rose Bowl win. | *Photograph by* NEIL LEIFER

1964 | MR. INTENSITY, Notre Dame coach Ara Parseghian watched the Fighting Irish's perfect season vanish in the haze against USC. | *Photograph by* SHEEDY & LONG

AUSTIN POWER

BY TIM LAYDEN

With a season that ranked among the best ever by a running back, Texas's Ricky Williams was closing in on the career rushing record.
—*from* SI, NOVEMBER 16, 1998

GREATNESS DOESN'T ALWAYS arrive with a flourish. Sometimes it grows quietly, revealing itself gradually to even those with the best view. Just last week Texas junior fullback Ricky Brown sat in a team meeting room at Memorial Stadium in Austin and looked to his right at senior tailback Ricky Williams. "I thought, There's a guy sitting next to me every day who's going down in history," recalls Brown. "In a few years I'm going to be telling my kids that I played with this guy, and man, those were some days."

For now, those *are* some days. College football history is dense with fabled running backs, from George Gipp to Tom Harmon to Doak Walker to O.J. Simpson to Archie Griffin to Tony Dorsett to Earl Campbell to Charles White to Herschel Walker to Bo Jackson to Barry Sanders. To that list it's time to add the name of Ricky Williams, who is in the midst of a season that ranks with that of any great running back in the college game.

What elevates Williams to this status is not just that he leads the nation in rushing, with 1,724 yards, and needs only 204 yards in his final two games to break Dorsett's NCAA Division I-A career record of 6,082. It is not just that he has scored more points (438) and more touchdowns (73) in his career than any college player in history. Or that, barring his abduction by aliens, he has wrapped up the Heisman Trophy. Or that he has been the most dominant player in the country since Labor Day weekend. ("The best, by far," says Oklahoma defensive coordinator Rex Ryan. "You hold your breath when he has the football; you're scared to death.") Or that he's as appealing to NFL franchises as a sweet stadium lease. ("The only flaw we've seen is that he can't hit the curveball," says Terry Bradway, head of player personnel for the Kansas City Chiefs, referring to Williams's struggles as a minor league baseball player in the Phillies organization.)

Rather, the circumstances of Williams's performance raise him into the elite class. Most running backs produce great seasons by playing for great teams (Simpson for USC in '68, Dorsett for Pittsburgh in '76, White for USC in '79, Eddie George for Ohio State in '95) or by blossoming unexpectedly, without reputation or pressure (Sanders for Oklahoma State in '88, Troy Davis for Iowa State in '95). Williams has done neither of those. He is playing for a Texas team that was in shambles last season and that hired a new coach, Mack Brown, only last December. Having rushed for 1,893 yards as a junior and finished fifth in the Heisman voting, Williams was Texas's only proven offensive option as this season opened. Yet the Longhorns are a stunning 7–2, with losses only to No. 2 Kansas State and No. 3 UCLA.

Texas developed a passing game because teams are fixated on stopping Williams. The Longhorns are consistently selling out its 80,216-seat stadium and have fallen back into the loving arms of desperate fans who have endured tradition withdrawal since the Darrell Royal era ended in 1977. There's more: Williams should already be gone. He would have been a top five pick in the NFL draft last spring, but he chose to return to Texas. He risks losing vast wealth nearly every time the Longhorns snap the ball. Last winter, fired Texas coach John Mackovic told Williams, "A running back can only take so many hits in his career." Williams doesn't disbelieve this, he simply disregards it. "It might be true," he said last week. "But even if I am costing myself years at the end of my career, I don't care. I'm having too much fun."

Every opposing team has hit him repeatedly—legally and otherwise. "The poor kid has got every defensive player on every team trying to rip his head off on every play, whether he's got the ball or not," says Brown. "I worry for him."

Williams plays with a number 37 decal on the back of his helmet, in memory of former SMU great Walker, whom Williams met last year while receiving the award that is named after him. Following Walker's death in September, Williams switched from jersey number 34 to number 37 for one game, against Oklahoma. After scoring a fourth-quarter touchdown he pounded the jersey, pointed to the sky and shouted, "That's for you, Doak!" It was a rare sentiment from a 21-year-old whose generation often regards history as insignificant.

Williams's performance must now be included in any historical discussion of the best seasons ever. More important, Williams is meeting the demands on his own list: He is better, he is a leader, and Dorsett's record should soon be toast. Williams is healthy and, for the first time in his career, fulfilled. "One thing," he says. "I'd like to play UCLA and Kansas State again."

Fulfilled, but never satisfied . . . .

A MIX of rumble and humble, Williams lassoed a Heisman, broke records, resuscitated the Longhorns and forged a reverent bond with Doak Walker.

1984 | SAILING OVER Georgia during a 27–0 win, Florida's rushing leader Neal Anderson helped the Gators rise to a No. 3 ranking by season's end. | *Photograph by* JOHN IACONO

The most famous (and most battered)
instrument in football history marched
into the Hall of Fame in 1995.

> **Artifacts**

Play It Again!

*The wildest ending ever in college football occurred
in the Big Game of 1982, when Cal's Kevin Moen,
completing a kickoff return after a series of five laterals
and with no time on the clock, had an end-zone run-
in with trombonist Gary Tyrrell, a member of the
Stanford band which had stormed the field believing
the Cardinal had already won the game. The officials
ruled the return a touchdown, the Bears had a 25–20
victory—and the Play has resounded ever since.*

Moen (28) ended the Stanford band's celebration and started his own after scoring the Bears' winning TD, then bowling over Tyrrell.

1982 | WITH BIG HAIR, a big grin and an even bigger arm, hometown hero Dan Marino became Pitt's greatest quarterback ever. | *Photograph by* MANNY MILLAN

1961 | ERNIE DAVIS of Syracuse was immersed in a whole new ball game, adding his autograph to pigskins signed by fellow All-Americas. | *Photograph by* BETTMANN/CORBIS

THE SMARTEST PLAYERS IN FOOTBALL

BY JOHN ED BRADLEY

They may look like big, slow brutes to the casual fan, but on and off the field, offensive linemen possess uncommon intellect.

—*from* SI, AUGUST 11, 2003

MOST SPECTATORS HARDLY pay them any mind, and those who do often wonder how they ever got so big and fat. Offensive linemen, their socks drooping down to their ankles, jerseys stretched tight over their guts, waddle to the line of scrimmage and briefly get in the way of the defense before falling to the ground and struggling to get back up. They come walking off the field and plop down on the bench, steam curling up around them like smoke from a barbecue pit.

Too bad fans can't peer inside the players' heads, because then they'd see complicated circuitry that operates without a kill switch. The behemoths of the offensive line are thinking men, forever processing defensive formations and alignments and calculating how to attack them, while simultaneously obsessing about things such as which foot to move first at the snap and how to position the hips for optimum leverage.

It is widely believed by coaches and NFL executives that offensive linemen are among the smartest players on the field. This notion is supported by the Wonderlic test given by NFL teams to prospective draft picks. In his 1984 book, *The New Thinking Man's Guide to Pro Football*, Paul Zimmerman revealed that over a five-year period offensive tackles (averaging 26 out of 50) and centers (25) scored the highest, and offensive guards (23) were fourth, behind quarterbacks (24). "Yeah, they're smarter," says Memphis defensive coordinator Joe Lee Dunn, who is in his 32nd season as a college coach. "They have to be. On defense we teach recklessness, whereas over on that side of the ball they're teaching things like finesse and footwork. Thirty years ago most offenses ran the I formation, and blocking was pretty straightforward. But these days you've got spread offenses and calls being made from the sideline. The passing game has taken over college offenses. When that happened, it got pretty complicated for offensive linemen."

Army coach Todd Berry said he and his staff reviewed film from last season and calculated that his offensive line had encountered at least 400 distinct defensive fronts. "Week in and week out you're facing a different system," he says. "You have to be able to respond to any variance you see across the defensive front, and then you have to be able to communicate that variance to everybody across the offense."

By studying nuances that fail to register with most casual observers, offensive linemen can see the future, and they can hear it as well. As he approaches the line of scrimmage, the center usually begins by declaring the defense and the position of the middle, or "mike," linebacker. For instance a noseguard playing straight over the center with two inside linebackers over the guards indicates a basic 50 defense, but put a mike linebacker over him and down linemen over the guards, and it's a 40 defense. Depending on the play that's been called in the huddle, the center makes his read and shouts out blocking schemes to both the play-side and backside guards, who in turn make their own calls to the tackles, one of whom then informs the tight end. Calls along the offensive front can change in a heartbeat if the defense shifts or the quarterback audibles. The defensive front is trained to attack a spot and then the ball, while the offensive front usually attacks the defense according to how the O-linemen interpret what they see. Dullards need not apply.

"If you've got a big kid who can really play, but he's not a great thinker," says South Florida coach Jim Leavitt, "you're better off putting him on the defensive side of the ball and telling him to just beat his guy off the line of scrimmage."

At most schools offensive linemen devote more hours to studying film and scouting reports than anyone else on the team, including the quarterbacks. "Quarterbacks are only concerned with their own position," says Kyle Young, a former Clemson center and three-time Academic All-America who is now a Tigers graduate assistant. "They get in the film room and hit it quick and they're done. But with the offensive line you have five different positions, and you end up studying film over and over for each of them. All that time together builds a strong work ethic, so you kind of become a team within the team. You feel connected to each other, and you want to pull your weight." . . .

A GRADE–A specimen of a brainy breed, Arkansas guard Brandon Burlsworth was a 1998 All-America and a solid student of marketing management.

2006 | FUMBLE-PROOFING himself, Auburn's Kenny Irons ran the chute of the Blaster while holding balls tricked out with sleeves that increased their slickness. | *Photograph by* TODD J. VAN EMST

> Training

Machine Dreams

Ever since Amos Alonzo Stagg invented the blocking sled and tackling dummy, coaches have used various contraptions to enhance performance. Some have worked. Others seemed like a good idea at the time

1938 | VILLANOVA COACH Maurice J. Smith got maximum resistance when he turned his Wildcats blocking-sled drill into a tractor pull.

1950s | THE BUCKING slingshot was designed to help Ohio State players, such as halfback Don Clark, to develop their leg drive.

1927 | THE CRASHMETER allowed Knute Rockne to gauge the blocks of Notre Dame players like John (Clipper) Smith.

1946 | A ROLLING oxygen tank was a breath of fresh air for (from left) Louis Surman, Tom Graham and Tony Beyer of Georgetown.

THE 2000s

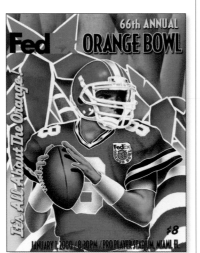

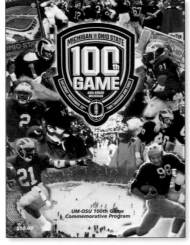

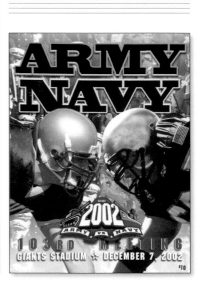

> THE ALL-DECADE TEAM

OFFENSE

TE	*Heath Miller* VIRGINIA
OL	*Joe Thomas* WISCONSIN
OL	*Jake Long* MICHIGAN
OL	*Shawn Andrews* ARKANSAS
OL	*Bryant McKinnie* MIAMI
C	*Jake Grove* VIRGINIA TECH
WR	*Larry Fitzgerald* PITTSBURGH
WR	*Dwayne Jarrett* USC
QB	*Vince Young* TEXAS
RB	*Reggie Bush* USC
RB	*Adrian Peterson* OKLAHOMA

DEFENSE

DL	*Dwight Freeney* SYRACUSE
DL	*Julius Peppers* NORTH CAROLINA
DL	*Glenn Dorsey* LSU
DL	*Tommie Harris* OKLAHOMA
LB	*Derrick Johnson* TEXAS
LB	*Paul Posluszny* PENN STATE
LB	*James Laurinaitis* OHIO STATE
DB	*Michael Huff* TEXAS
DB	*Ed Reed* MIAMI
DB	*Jimmy Williams* VIRGINIA TECH
DB	*Roy Williams* OKLAHOMA

>NICKNAMES<

Carnell [Cadillac] Williams ^
Keith [The Teeth] Adams
Rodney [Boss] Bailey
Ronnie [The Hummer] Brown
James [Buster] Davis
Noel [Skittles] Devine
Glenn [Big House] Dorsey
Derrick [Noodle] Hamilton
Terry [Tank] Johnson
Adam [Pacman] Jones
Jared [The Hefty Lefty] Lorenzen
Dulymus [Deuce] McAllister
Darren [Run DMC] McFadden
Marvin [Snoop] Minnis
Adrian [All-Day] Peterson
Matt [Iceman] Ryan
George [Sackman] Selvie
Mosiula [Lofa] Tatupu
Chris [Beanie] Wells
LenDale [Thunder] White
Reggie [Lightning] Bush

HEISMAN TROPHY WINNER

'00	CHRIS WEINKE Florida State
'01	ERIC CROUCH Nebraska
'02	CARSON PALMER USC
'03	JASON WHITE Oklahoma
'04	MATT LEINART USC
'05	REGGIE BUSH USC
'06	TROY SMITH Ohio State
'07	TIM TEBOW Florida

RUSHING LEADER

	YARDS PER GAME
LaDAINIAN TOMLINSON TCU	196.2
CHANCE KRETSCHMER Nevada	157.5
LARRY JOHNSON Penn State	160.5
PATRICK COBBS North Texas	152.7
JAMARIO THOMAS North Texas	180.1
DeANGELO WILLIAMS Memphis	178.5
GARRETT WOLFE Northern Illinois	148.3
KEVIN SMITH Central Florida	183.4

PASSING LEADER

	EFFICIENCY
BART HENDRICKS Boise State	170.6
REX GROSSMAN Florida	170.8
BRAD BANKS Iowa	157.1
PHILIP RIVERS N.C. State	170.5
STEFAN LEFORS Louisville	181.7
RUDY CARPENTER Arizona State	175.0
COLT BRENNAN Hawaii	186.0
SAM BRADFORD Oklahoma	176.5

>> THE DECADE'S DYNASTIES

USC
QBs Carson Palmer (2002) and Matt Leinart ('04), and RB Reggie Bush ('05) earned Heismans as coach Pete Carroll resuscitated his career and the Trojans program with two national titles ('03 and '04) and a 34-game winning streak.

LSU
The Bayou Bengals were the only team to win two BCS titles: in 2003 under Nick Saban, and in '07 under Les Miles. Quarterback JaMarcus Russell and defensive linemen Glenn Dorsey were real Tigers as LSU garnered six bowl wins.

Ohio State
Three times in Jim Tressel's first seven years as Ohio State coach the Buckeyes played for the BCS championship, and they won it in 2002. During the decade Vernon Gholston, James Laurinaitis, A.J. Hawk and Mike Doss anchored a D that has allowed a nation-low 15.7 points per game.

Florida
From the final days of the Steve Spurrier tenure and continuing into the Urban Meyer era that featured the 2006 BCS champions and the first sophomore Heisman winner (QB Tim Tebow, '07), the Gators have been a perennial power in the nation's strongest conference.

Appalachian State >
The Mountaineers' win at Michigan in 2007 was a stunner but no fluke: From '05 through '07, coach Jerry Moore strung together three straight Football Championship Series (formerly Division I-AA) titles for App State, the first school to pull off that trifecta in the 30-year history of the tournament.

Dexter Jackson and Appalachian State scored the big shocker at the Big House.

> EPIC GAMES

<Oklahoma *vs.* Boise State
January 1, 2007 • FIESTA BOWL

In their first BCS Bowl game, the Broncos, Western Athletic Conference champs, squandered an 18-point third quarter lead over the Sooners, then redeemed themselves with a 50-yard hook and lateral at the end of regulation, a fourth-and-two option pass thrown by a receiver in OT, and a Statue of Liberty play for a two-point conversion and a 43–42 win.

Appalachian State *vs.* Michigan
September 1, 2007

The 109,218 fans at the Big House couldn't have dreamed that the fifth-ranked Wolverines would lose their opener to the Mountaineers. But the two-time Division I-AA champions scored 21 points in the second quarter, and Corey Lynch blocked a 37-yard field goal with six seconds left to allow State to pull off a 34–32 upset.

USC *vs.* Texas
January 4, 2006 • ROSE BOWL

The Trojans, riding a 34-game winning streak and seeking a third straight national title behind Heisman Trophy winners Matt Leinart and Reggie Bush, ran into Longhorns QB Vince Young, who rolled up 467 yards of total offense and three rushing TDs, including an eight-yard run with 19 seconds left to give Texas a 41–38 comeback victory.

> CAMPUS CULTURE

YOU'VE GOT TO . . .

READ IT: *Fast Food Nation*, Eric Schlosser; *The Da Vinci Code*, Dan Brown; *The Tipping Point*, Malcolm Gladwell; *Harry Potter* series, J.K. Rowling; *The Kite Runner*, Khaled Hosseini

HEAR IT: Modest Mouse, The White Stripes, Black Eyed Peas, Kelly Clarkson, Snoop Dogg, Kanye West, Tim McGraw, 50 Cent

SEE IT: *Napoleon Dynamite, Borat, An Inconvenient Truth, Lord of the Rings* and sequels, *Entourage, American Idol, Family Guy, Survivor, The Sopranos, Brokeback Mountain, Sex and the City*

"Major combat operations . . . have ended. In the battle of Iraq, the United States and our allies have prevailed."
—*President George W. Bush, while standing under a* MISSION ACCOMPLISHED *banner on the USS Abraham Lincoln, May 1, 2003*

DISCUSS IT: Iraq, global warming, Barack Obama, hanging chads, Darfur, Britney Spears

HAVE IT: Wii, iPod, tats, Blackberry, ringtones, Tivo, Facebook/MySpace page

WEAR IT: Burberry, bling, polos, camo, designer sweats

DO IT: Blog, The South Beach diet, Texas Hold 'Em, Guitar Hero, crunk

DEAL WITH IT: 9/11, gas prices, Hurricane Katrina, 'roids

Strum along with Judy: By amping up the videogame volume, every dorm could have a Guitar Hero.

> WORLD'S SMARTEST GUY

STEPHEN WOLFRAM British computer scientist, physicist and mathematician whose 2002 book, *A New Kind of Science*, established a scientific foundation for complexity theory and artificial life.

> BY THE NUMBERS

387.9 | Yards of total offense per game by Hawaii QB Colt Brennan, the highest career average ever.

18 | Consecutive games in which Pittsburgh receiver Larry Fitzgerald caught at least one TD pass, an NCAA record.

117 | Games through 2007 between Minnesota and Wisconsin, the most often-played rivalry in college football.

45 | Millions of dollars NBC paid Notre Dame for the rights to broadcast Irish home games from 2005 to '10.

9 | Division III championships by Mount Union, including five since 2000.

55 | Bowl appearances for Alabama through 2007. No other school has been to more than 47 postseason games.

453 | Games won by John Gagliardi through 2007 as coach at St. John's University and Carroll College.

392 | Margin by which the 112,118 present at the 2003 Ohio State–Michigan game at Ann Arbor exceeded the previous attendance record.

INNOVATOR

Urban Meyer At Bowling Green, Utah and Florida, Meyer's shotgun-based attack puts pressure on defenses, allowing multiskilled QBs (like Alex Smith and Tim Tebow) to exploit the vast open spaces created by his spread-option offense.

c. 1910 | SOME CADETS (striped sleeves) were equipped with headgear against Harvard, but one West Pointer still suffered a mortal head injury in the '09 battle with the Crimson, prompting Army to cancel its remaining games. | *Photograph by* BROWN BROTHERS

1996 | HIS FOOT went one way, the rest of him another as Colorado's Rae Carruth put a twist on one of his season's 54 catches. | *Photograph by* RONALD C. MODRA

1965 | TEXAS TECH back Donny Anderson, nicknamed "the Golden Palomino," kicked up his heels after snaring a pass against Baylor. | *Photograph by* WALTER IOOSS JR.

1997 | PLAYERS NEVER appreciated the fans more than they did on the sideline of the steamy L.A. Coliseum during USC's 14–7 season-opening loss to Florida State. | *Photograph by* ROBERT BECK

1989 | UCLA DEFENSIVE TACKLE Jon Pryor couldn't just walk away in frustration after a 10–10 tie with USC. | *Photograph by* DOUGLAS KIRKLAND

1989 | INDIANA COACH Bill Mallory consoled star back Anthony Thompson after a heartbreaking loss to Purdue. | *Photograph by* WILLIAM STRODE

2002 | WHERE'S WALDO? Who knows, but quarterback Craig Krenzel (16) could be found bobbing in a sea of delirious Buckeyes boosters after Ohio State clinched a berth in the BCS title game with a 14–9 win over archrival Michigan. | *Photograph by* DAVID BERGMAN